Singapore Math® Sourcebook

An Introduction to the World's Top-Scoring Math Program

W9-CHS-744

competent & confident

Cassandra Turner

Cassy@SingaporeMathSource.com

math home enjoyment = homework

entrance test
Placement - bottom of home page
- getting started - U.S ed. placement ed

Math Anxiety Scale

Answer the following questions:

1 - Strongly Agree; 2 - Agree; 3 - Neither; 4 - Disagree; 5 -Strongly disagree.

		1	2	3	4	5
1	I recall math classes in school fondly.					
2	I was happy to answer questions posed during math class.					
3	I recall being comfortable asking questions during math class.					
4	I enjoy teaching math.					
5	I understand math and feel comfortable answering questions posed by students.					
6	I enjoy preparing math lesson plans.					
7	I was comfortable in school solving math problems in front of the class.					
8	I describe my math skills as average or above average.					
9	I am confident in my ability to solve math problems.					

Now total your score from the above chart.

36 – 45	You've got math anxiety to the max!
27 – 35	You've got some fears about math.
18 – 26	Not too bad, but you've got a bit of the bug.
9 – 17	Math anxiety is not an issue for you. Congratulations!

Combating Math Anxiety

"Evidence suggests that math anxiety results more from the way the subject is presented than from the subject itself."

- Greenwood

"Mathematics anxiety arises when one stage (of mathematical understanding) is unheedingly skipped...many of the layers of mathematical knowledge are so elementary that they are often easy to miss. When this happens, an attempt is made to establish a new layer on top of the missing one, neither the teacher nor the student can discern the origin of the problem. The student hears something that is meaningless to him since he is "probably not yet ready'."
— Aharoni

Children don't hate math. They hate being confused by math.

Myths about Math

There are several myths about math that are often associated with the development of math anxiety. Research has shown that none are true, but many people believe them and may struggle with math anxiety:

- **Men are better at math than women.** This is a stereotype that is often reinforced by society, including by teachers, parents, and guidance counselors.

- **There is a "best" or "correct" way to complete math problems.** There are many ways to get to a correct answer in a math problem. Think about the many different ways people figure out a tip for a restaurant bill, or how much they will save on a sale item.

- **You have to have a "mathematical mind" to understand math.** People are not born with different types of brains. Myths such as this one discourage people from finding the learning tools that work best for them, and cause people to give up on learning math.

        -Excerpted from "Developing Math Confidence. University of Florida Counseling Center

From the National Mathematics Advisory Panel:

- Positive attitudes about mathematics education are important to student success.

- Research shows that a child's **goals for and beliefs about learning** are related to his or her performance in mathematics.

- Students who believe that their **hard work makes them "smarter"** are more likely to try harder in mathematics, and their efforts result in better performance. On the other hand, students who believe that intelligence is inborn generally do not achieve as well, and they do not take full advantage of feedback or constructive criticism regarding their performance.

*Brochures for parents are available **free** from the following website:*
http://www.ed.gov/parents/academic/help/hyc.html.

What is Singapore Math?

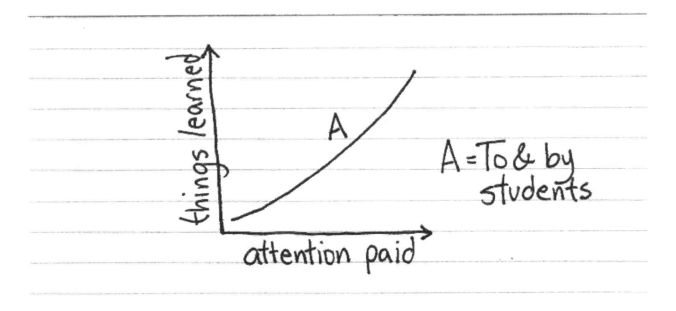

$A = To$ & by students

things learned

attention paid

A Brief History of Singapore

Singapore is a tiny island country in Southeast Asia, measuring approximately 200 square miles. The name "Singapore" comes from the Sanskrit words *singa pura,* meaning "lion city". The legend goes that Sang Nila Utama, while hunting on this island on the way to Malacca, saw a lion in the forest, and so named the island for the lion. In fact, a very famous statue in Singapore is the Merlion, which has the head of a lion and the body of a fish, and recalls the legend of Sang Nila Utama.

Singapore was a fishing village until it was colonized by the British in August 1819. Sir Thomas Raffles landed on the island on January 28, 1819, and immediately realized its potential as a trading post. During World War II, Japan occupied Singapore. In 1945, the island was returned to Great Britain. Finally, in 1965, Singapore gained independence.

Modern day Singapore is a mix of cultures and religious beliefs. Most of the people who live in Singapore are of three different nationalities: Chinese, Malay, and Indian. When Sir Thomas Stamford Bingley Raffles was colonizing the island he divided the nationalities by creating Chinatown; Little India; and the Malayan section. Today, however, people of all nationalities and beliefs live together, work together, and attend school together.

The History of Singapore Math

A relatively small and densely populated island, Singapore's only **natural resource is their people.** The country has chosen to focus on building strong Singaporean citizens beginning with their earliest education. The mathematics curriculum was developed with this goal in mind. The first primary mathematics curriculum was developed in 1981 by the Curriculum Development Institute of Singapore. In Singapore, it is simply referred to as "maths". The term "Singapore Math®" refers to the Marshall Cavendish Primary Mathematics series of materials used in the U.S. and several other countries.

The 1981 curriculum focused on basic content. This curriculum was revised in 1992 to make it a problem solving curriculum. The Primary Mathematics (2nd Edition) was based on the 1992 curriculum.

The Primary Mathematics (3rd Edition) series was based on a reduced syllabus in 1994. In 1999, Singapore's Ministry of Education decided to reduce the content in the curriculum up to 30% for most subjects.

Singapore Math in the United States

In 1998, the first books were imported from Singapore for use in this country (Primary Mathematics 3rd Edition). These books were written in British English and contained Singaporean money and only metric measurement. The U.S. Edition was created in 2001 and included American measurement and money. In 2007, an edition aligned to California State Standards was created. Referred to as the "Standards Edition", it is likely that this version will undergo alignment to the Common Core in the future.

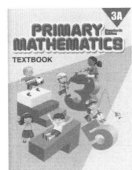

The most recent series published in the United States is Math in Focus by Great Source Publishing. This series was adapted from My Pals Are Here, currently in use in Singapore and includes the National Council of Teachers of Mathematics (NCTM) Focal Points as well as Common Core State Standards.

Singapore Leads the World

In 1995, Singapore participated in the Third International Mathematics and Science Study (TIMSS). This was the largest and most ambitious international study of student achievement ever conducted. In 1994–95, it was conducted at five grade levels in more than 40 countries.

Students were tested in mathematics and science and extensive information about the teaching and learning of mathematics and science was collected from students, teachers, and school principals. Altogether, the TIMSS tested more than half a million students worldwide and administered questionnaires to thousands of teachers and school principals.

Between the creation of a math curriculum in 1981 and the TIMSS testing in 1995, Singapore students climbed to the top in the world.

In fact, Singapore has ranked #1 or #2 on the first three TIMSS (now called *Trends* in International Mathematics and Science Study) administered (1995, 1999, 2003, 2007).

Most telling on the TIMSS 2011 is that 43% of Singaporean students met **advanced** benchmarks, while only 13% of U.S. students reached that same level.

Further information can be found at http://nces.ed.gov/pubs2011

Trends in Math and Science Study

	Fourth-grade		Eighth-grade

2011 International Test Results

1	**Singapore**	**606**	1	Korea, Republic of	613
2	Korea, Republic of	605	2	**Singapore**	611
3	Hong Kong	603	3	Chinese Taipei	609
11	**United States**	**541**		**United States**	**509**
	Scale average	500		Scale average	500

2007 International Test Results

1	Hong Kong	607	1	Chinese Taipei	598
2	**Singapore**	**599**	2	Korea, Republic of	597
3	Chinese Taipei	576	**3**	**Singapore**	**593**
11	**United States**	**529**		**United States**	**508**
	Scale average	500		Scale average	500

2003 International Test Results

1	**Singapore**	**594**	**1**	**Singapore**	**605**
2	Hong Kong SAR	575	2	Korea, Republic of	589
3	Japan	565	3	Hong Kong SAR	586
12	**United States**	**518**		**United States**	**504**
	Scale average	495		Scale average	466

1999 International Test Results

Fourth Grade Testing was not Conducted in 1999			**1**	**Singapore**	**604**
			2	Korea, Republic of	587
			3	Chinese Taipei	585
			19	**United States**	**502**
				Scale average	487

1995 International Test Results

1	**Singapore**	**625**	**1**	**Singapore**	**643**
2	Korea	611	2	Korea	607
3	Japan	597	3	Japan	605
7	**United States**	**545**		**United States**	**500**
	International Average	529		International Average	513

Percent of students meeting corresponding benchmark

Advanced International Benchmark - 625

Students can apply their understanding and knowledge in a variety of relatively complex situations and explain their reasoning. They can solve a variety of multi-step word problems involving whole numbers including proportions. Students at this level show an increasing understanding of fractions and decimals. Students can apply geometric knowledge of a range of two- and three-dimensional shapes in a variety of situations. They can draw a conclusion from data in a table and justify their conclusion

High International Benchmark - 550

Students can apply their knowledge and understanding to solve problems. Students can solve word problems involving operations with whole numbers. They can use division in a variety of problem situations. They can use their understanding of place value to solve problems. Students can extend patterns to find a later specified term. Students demonstrate understanding of line symmetry and geometric properties. Students can interpret and use data in tables and graphs to solve problems. They can use information in pictographs and tally charts to complete bar graphs.

Intermediate International Benchmark – 475

Students can apply basic mathematical knowledge in straightforward situations. Students at this level demonstrate an understanding of whole numbers and some understanding of fractions. Students can visualize three-dimensional shapes from two-dimensional representations. They can interpret bar graphs, pictographs, and tables to solve simple problems.

Low International Benchmark – 400

Students have some basic mathematical knowledge. e. Students can add and subtract whole numbers. They have some recognition of parallel and perpendicular lines, familiar geometric shapes, and coordinate maps. They can read and complete simple bar graphs and tables.

- IEA's Trends in International Mathematics and Science Study (TIMSS) 2011

Curricula from top scoring countries on TIMSS share 3 characteristics:

1. **Coherence** - The content is not a bunch of arbitrary topics — it follows the structure of the discipline. Students are expected to understand the basic before the complex.

2. **Focus** - How many topics are covered at each grade level — "Mile wide vs. inch deep"

3. **Rigor** - As one moves across the grades the complexity goes up. Sixth graders should not be learning multiplication facts. Students are expected to reason about mathematical concepts.

Findings from the American Institutes for Research® Study

Funded by the U.S. Department of Education, the American Institutes for Research (AIR) conducted a study of schools using Singapore Math® in Massachusetts, New Jersey and Maryland. The study, "What the United States Can Learn from Singapore's World - Class Mathematics System (and what Singapore can learn from the United States)", identified major differences between the mathematics frameworks, textbooks, assessments, and teacher preparation in both countries. The results of the study were released in 2005.

"It is **unreasonable to assume that Singaporean students have mathematical abilities inherently superior to those of U.S. students**; rather, there must be something about the system that Singapore has developed to teach mathematics that is better than the system we use in the United States. That's why it's important to take a closer look, and see how the U.S can learn and how the U.S can improve."

- "Singapore Mathematics textbooks can produce significant boosts in achievement."

- "What the US needs overall are the sound features of the Singapore Mathematics system."

- "The Singapore program provides rich problem sets that give students many and varied opportunities to apply the concepts they have learned."

- Singapore's textbooks build deep understanding of mathematical concepts while traditional U.S. textbooks rarely get beyond definitions and formulas.

Full report available: http://www.air.org

Five Factors to Singapore's Success

When asked why Singapore has ranked #1 in the world on the 1995, 1999 and 2003 TIMSS tests, members of the Singaporean Ministry of Education said, "In our country we have five factors which all work together to account for this success:

1. Qualified and dedicated teachers
2. Well-managed schools
3. Subject banding
4. High expectations on the part of parents, teachers, and students
5. A sound curriculum

Qualified and Dedicated Teachers

The Ministry of Education wants only dedicated teachers. In order ensure this, when a teacher is employed, a contract is signed in which the teacher agrees to a minimum of three years in the profession. Any teacher who violates this agreement must repay all earned income from teaching. Prior to entering University to become a teacher, students are placed in a classroom to get a hands-on feeling for the career.

Teachers are well respected in Singapore and are continually offered positions for advancement. A primary school teacher may advance to a secondary math (or other) position, department head, mentor teacher or they may look to an administrative track. Many opportunities are available and teachers are encouraged to advance. (They are also given 100 hours of continuing education annually!)

Well-managed schools

Teachers are observed by the head of the maths department of their school on a regular basis as well as by school principals and administration. A struggling teacher receives support from mentor teachers, heads of department, and administration. Teachers in elementary school generally teach 3 – 4 hours per day, and only three subjects: maths, English, and either "mother tongue" or science (beginning in fourth grade). The rest of their time is spent correcting all of the students' work, meeting/planning with other teachers, etc.

Subject Banding

Beginning in grade 4, students are placed in similar-ability groups for maths and English. Teachers of homogeneous groups can match the pace of instruction to the children's learning pace. The strongest teachers are placed with the groups who struggle the most. In the 5th and 6th grades, students who struggle in mathematics take a "Foundations" track that focuses on the most basic mathematics.

High expectations

High achievement is prized by the Singaporean society. Math ability is believed to be more a matter of hard work than of innate ability. Remediation is begun two months into first grade for any student who is behind his peers. 50% or more of elementary school parents pay for private tutors so that their students can do BETTER, not because they are behind. Presents to children are often math workbooks.

Singapore, like many other countries, has high stakes testing that determines which route in life a student will be able to take. At the end of sixth grade, all students take the Primary School Leaving Exam ("PSLE").

The results of this test determine in which secondary track the student will be placed. If a student demonstrates great success in the early years of secondary school (4 or 5 years, depending on which track the student is in), the student may get another chance to pass the test allowing admittance to the university.

Weapons of Math Destruction ™

www.weaponsofmathdestruction.com © Oak Norton

_ ɔ, what's so special about the Singapore Curriculum?

> "Since 1991, the framework of the Singapore mathematics curriculum has been articulated in a pentagon model...Mathematics departments are well aware that 'the primary aim of the mathematics curriculum is to enable students to develop their ability in mathematical problem solving' and that the attainment of this aim is dependent on the five inter-related components of Concepts, Skills, Processes, Attitudes and Metacognition."

Teaching Secondary School Mathematics: A Resource Book

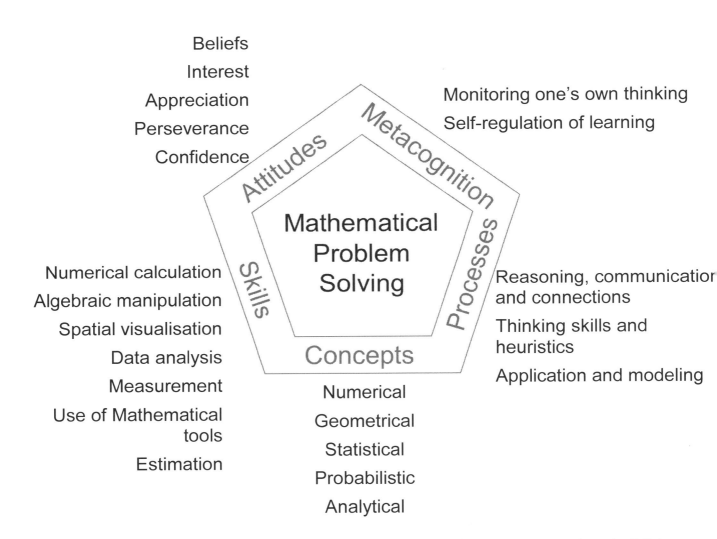

- Ministry of Education Primary Mathematics Syllabus

Big ideas in Singapore Mathematics

"Mathematics is an excellent vehicle for the development and improvement of a person's intellectual competence in logical reasoning, spatial visualisation, analysis and abstract thought. Students develop numeracy, reasoning, thinking skills, and problem solving skills through the learning and application of mathematics....

...Mathematics is also a subject of enjoyment and excitement, which offers students opportunities for creative work and moments of enlightenment and joy. When ideas are discovered and insights gained, students are spurred to pursue mathematics beyond the classroom walls."

-Ministry of Education Primary Mathematics Syllabus 2007

Number Sense:

Number sense implies having a deep understanding of mathematical concepts, making sense of various mathematical ideas, as well as developing mathematical connections and applications. Students with strong number sense can make connections between their knowledge and newly learned mathematical concepts and skills. In general, they know how to make sense of numbers, how to apply them, and are confident that their problem solving processes will enable them to arrive at solutions.

Making Connections/Finding Patterns

Connections refer to the ability to see and make linkages among mathematical ideas, between mathematics and other subjects, and between mathematics and everyday life. These connections help students make sense of what they learn in mathematics.

Communication

Communication refers to the ability to use mathematical language to express mathematical ideas and arguments precisely, concisely and logically. It helps students develop their own understanding of mathematics and sharpen their mathematical thinking.

Visualization

*"Manipulation of materials is crucial. In order to think, children in the **concrete operational** stage need to have objects in front of them that are easy to handle, or else to visualize objects that have been handled and that are easily imagined without any real effort."*   - Piaget

Singapore Curriculum recognizes three stages of learning: Concrete, Pictorial, and Abstract. Although the most challenging stage for a classroom teacher may be the concrete, it is not to be shortchanged.

The concrete and pictorial stages are the **bridge to abstract computation.** A list of manipulatives is available on page 93.

Concrete items that may be used in a classroom include:

- base 10 blocks
- scales
- thermometers
- cards

- **number disks**
- dominos
- meter sticks
- origami paper

- counters
- geoboards
- dice
- hula hoops

Pictorial items may include:

- pictures of items
- sets

- drawings
- models

- graphs
- number lines and timeline

Bar modeling is the heuristic emphasized in the Singapore Mathematics curriculum as a representative tool for students to use when problem solving.

Variation

Zoltan Dienes' perceptual variability principle suggests that conceptual learning is maximized when children are exposed to a concept through a variety of physical contexts or embodiments. Providing multiple experiences, not the same experience **many** times, and using a variety of materials is designed to promote abstraction of a mathematical concept. When children are given opportunities to see a concept in different ways and under different conditions, they are more likely to understand that concept in different ways, under different conditions.

This avoids students ascribing inappropriate attributes to a concept. Lack of diversity in mathematical examples leads to "fixation".

Ex: Orientation is not an attribute of "triangle-ness'.

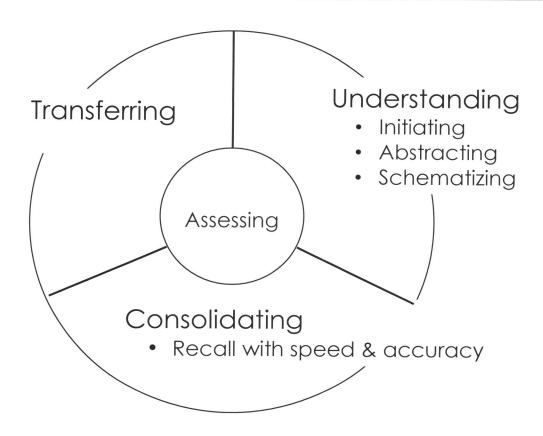

The Singaporean teaching model includes a four-part activity model. Planning for instruction should include all types of activities.

The **understanding** phase consists of the initial lessons of any concept new to students. The introduction of model drawing and learning how to draw basic models occur during this phase.

Drill and practice are done during the **consolidation** phase. After students have an understanding of the skill or concept, 10-minute review activities should be scheduled at the start of class in the weeks after a key topic or concept has been introduced. Flashcards, games, worksheets, textbook mental math, etc. are all examples of practice activities. Model drawing is not typically used to help students' fluency.

Model drawing is most typical of the **transfer** phase of instruction. Students should have a good understanding of the concept and skills necessary. Students then apply their knowledge in new situations, including solving routine and non-routine problems.

Mental Math

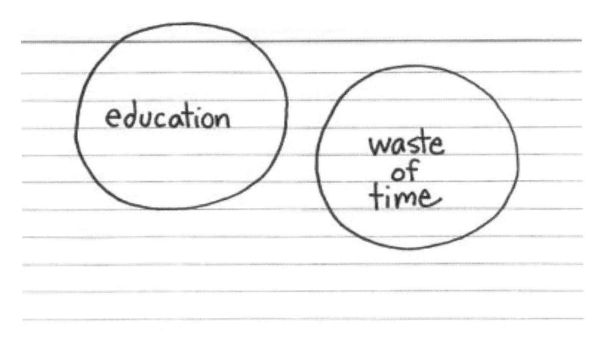

Why Mental Math?

Mental Math ability is considered a hallmark of number sense! It also emphasizes an understanding of place value and the distributive, commutative and associative properties.

The ability to do basic calculations in one's head develops the flexible thinking required by most state and the Common Core State Standards.

Mental Math:
- ✓ develops number sense

- ✓ provides practice with place value skills.

- ✓ creates deep understanding of the distributive property.

- ✓ is fun!

- ✓ gives immediate feedback on student understanding.

- ✓ develops memory and mental organization skills.

- ✓ allows auditory learners a chance at success.

- ✓ can be done anytime & anywhere...without special materials...in the car, on the bus, in the lunch line...

The ability to work calculations in your head is a "necessary prerequisite for the arithmetic of fractions and decimals, and (these skills) help bridge the gap between arithmetic and algebra". (Parker & Baldridge)

Incorporating Mental Math in the Classroom

1. Magic Thumb
2. Sprints
3. Number Strings
4. Skip counting
5. Text lessons
6. Games (Ping! Beep!, Salute)
7. I Have — Who Has?
8. ??

Because mental math is so crucial in the Singapore Math materials, **each class period should have mental math components.**

Remember, mental math **can include pencil and paper, as long as the actual calculation is done mentally** and only the solution is written on the paper. The more practice a student has with mental math, the more automatic it will become.

*This is one area in which parents can be extremely helpful. They can help students *practice to mastery!*

Anytime is a great time for math!

How can you incorporate mental math activities into...

- Spelling
- Grammar
- Reading
- Social Sciences
- Physical Education
- Calendar - In the earlier grades, calendar time is an excellent time to incorporate math. For example, "Today is Tuesday, March 7. How many days will it be until March 17? What day was it 12 days ago?"

- Dismissal - Don't let students out to recess for free. As they're lined up, ask each one a mental math fact. If a child is unable to answer in a reasonable period of time, have the child go to the end of the line and try again.

- Science - Extend Science units to incorporate math. Temperature is a simple example: "Today it is 82 degrees. Tonight the temperature is supposed to dip to 64 degrees. What is the difference between the two temperatures?"

- Lunch - If pizza is being served, excellent time to assess understanding of fractional pieces. Example: "I see that this pizza is cut into eight pieces. They look to be the same size. What fractional part of the pizza is one slice?" (1/8) "How many pieces of pizza make up ½ of the pizza?" (4)

- Cartography - Older students can begin basic cartography. Many students enjoy fantasy or Role Playing Games where they can create their own worlds.

- Recess - Add math-type games that children can play during recess.

  - Large outdoor chess sets are excellent for developing spatial skills.

  - Hopscotch where children have to add or multiply numbers they land on, depending on directions from you.

- Art - angles, measurement, proportionality all lend themselves to mathematical activities.

- Music - Sing songs using math facts as the lyrics, patterns in music relate to patterns in mathematics.

Why don't we just use a calculator?

Calculators are fine for challenging computations. The ability to calculate relies on an understanding of principles and principles are learned through practice! The basic skills of rearranging numbers and understanding place value are simply not developed when using a calculator. Students who rely on calculators for basic computation miss these skills. By skipping these important layers, students are hampered in their further mathematical study. Skipping mathematical layers also leads to anxiety.

As a teacher, you need to be able to assess students' understanding and work quickly. Will you be carrying a calculator?

Image copyright © Oak Norton and has been reproduced with permission.

Weapons of Math Destruction ™

I want you to use this crutch for the next 70 years

I want you to use this calculator for the next 70 years

2+1=

GET OUT YOUR CALCULATOR

Bob Bonham

www.weaponsofmathdestruction.com   © Oak Norton

Fluency

Procedural fluency involves:

1. Accuracy – The fact must be correct.
2. Efficiency – 3-5 seconds.

3. Flexibility – Understanding of process.

Common Core Required Fluency by Grade	
K	Add/subtract within 5
1	Add/subtract within 10
2	Add/subtract within 20[1] Add/subtract within 100 (pencil and paper)
3	Multiply/divide within 100[2] Add/subtract within 1000
4	Add/subtract within 1,000,000
5	Multi-digit multiplication
6	Multi-digit division Multi-digit decimal operations
[1] By end of year, know from memory all sums of two one-digit numbers [2] By end of year, know from memory all products of two one-digit numbers	

Number Bonds

Number Bonds lay the foundation for the Model Method with the focus on the part-part-whole relationship in early grades:

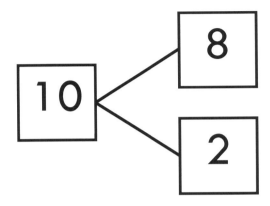

10 can be broken down into 8 and 2

10 − 2 = ?

2 and __ make 10.

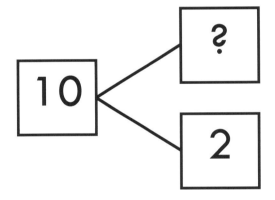

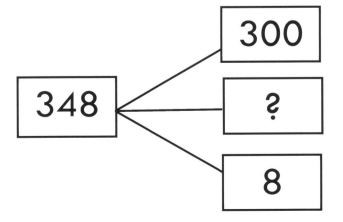

300 + _____ + 8

Kindergarten introduces the concept with multiple variations. First, pictures of children (concrete) then bar models (pictorial) finally, an informal introduction to addition using the term "and" (abstract).

The Number Bond concept is used to teach addition and subtraction throughout first grade. As a tool, it helps students visualize connections to other concepts:

Third Grade unit: Money

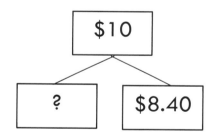

Fourth Grade unit: Decimal Division

$$12.20 \div 4 = ?$$

12   20 hundredths

Fourth Grade unit: Fractions

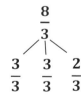

$$\frac{8}{3}$$

$\frac{3}{3}$ $\frac{3}{3}$ $\frac{2}{3}$

"This consistent use of a single powerful model provides a unifying pedagogical structure entirely missing in U.S. mathematics programs."

-Steven Leinwand

Mental Math Methods

Although many strategies will be discussed, students should be encouraged to use any strategy in mental calculation, including strategies not yet introduced. Number bonds are shown here to illustrate these strategies, but students should not be required to draw these number bonds.

Decomposing and composing: Taking numbers apart and putting them together. Most used to build and take apart bundles of 10.

Rearranging numbers: using the distributive property to find compatible numbers.

Compatible numbers: numbers that can be combined to make a simpler problem

$$64 + 27 + 36 = 100 + 27$$
$$2 \times 35 \times 5 = (2 \times 5) \times 35 = 350$$
$$104 \div 8 = (80 + 24) \div 8 = 10 + 3 = 13$$

Compensation: Another way to make a simpler problem

Addition:	$98 + 37 = 100 + 35$
Subtraction:	$96 - 37 = 99 - 40$
Multiplication:	$25 \times 16 = 100 \times 4$
Division:	$360 \div 20 = 180 \div 10$

Splitting numbers and left to right calculations:

$$427 + 306 = 700 + (27 + 6)$$
$$6 \times 125 = (6 \times 100) + (6 \times 25)$$

SOME MENTAL MATH STRATEGIES

Decomposing and composing: Taking numbers apart and putting them together. Most used to build and take apart bundles of 10.	Use ten frames and number bonds
Rearranging and compatible numbers. Using the "Any-order" and distributive properties.	$40 + 27 + 60 = 40 + 60 + 27 = 127$ $2 \times 224 \times 5 = (2 \times 5) \times 224 = 2240$ $52 \div 4 = (40 + 12) \div 4 = 10 + 3 = 13$

Compensation
 	
    Addition: One addend gives to the other:
	$98 + 27 = 100 + 25$
	
	    $2 \quad 25$

Subtraction: Change the minuend and the subtrahend by the same amount. (Same difference strategy)	$76 - 30$ $+2 \qquad +2$ $74 - 28$
Multiplication: One factor gives to the other	$50 \times 14 = 50 \times (2 \times 7)$ Double 50, halve 7: 100×7
Division: multiply (or divide) the dividend and divisor by the same number. (Double – double strategy	$135 \div 5 = 270 \div 10 = 27$ $640 \div 20 = 320 \div 10 = 32$
Left to right calculations focusing on place value.	$207 + 108 = 200 + 100 + 7 + 8$ $412 \times 3 = (400 \times 3) + (10 \times 3) + (2 \times 3)$ $\qquad = 1200 + 30 + 6 = 1236$

The following strategies are taught in grades 1-3 in the Singapore Mathematics materials. They are summed up here for teachers working with older grade levels.

(From: Teacher's Guide Standards Edition 3A: Unit 2 - Addition and Subtraction and MathsExpress: Speed Maths Strategies Level 2 & 3)

Addition

➢ Add two 1-digit numbers whose sum is greater than 10 by making a 10.

$$7 + 5 =$$

➢ Add tens to 2-digit numbers by adding the tens.

$$48 + 20 =$$

➢ Add a 1-digit number to a 2-digit number; adding the ones results in a number greater than 10 by making a 10 or by using basic addition facts.

$$68 + 5 =$$

➤ Add a 2-digit number to a 2-digit number by making a ten.

        48 + 25 =

Add a 2-digit number to a 2-digit number by adding the next ten and then subtract appropriate number of ones.

        48 + 25 =

➤ Add a number close to 100 by making 100.

        57 + 98 =

➤ Add a number close to 100 by first adding 100 and then subtracting the difference.

        57 + 98 =

        54 + 80 =

Subtraction

➢ Subtract tens from 2-digit numbers by subtracting the tens.

$$48 - 20 =$$

➢ Subtract a 1-digit number from a 2-digit number when there are not enough ones by:
  ○ subtracting from 10
  ○ using basic subtraction facts

$$65 - 8 =$$

➢ Subtract a 2 digit number from a 2 digit number by subtracting from the nearest ten.

$$75 - 38 =$$

➢ Subtract a 2 digit number from a 2 digit number by subtracting the next ten and then adding back in the appropriate number of ones.

$$75 \quad - 38 =$$

➤ Subtract a number close to 100 by subtracting 100 and then adding back the difference.

457 – 98 =

➤ Subtract a number without regrouping

1000 – 364 =

➤ Subtract using compensation

47 – 19 =

Multiplication

➢ Multiply a 2 digit number by a 1-digit number by expanded notation.

        13 x 4 =

➢ Multiply a 2 digit number by a 1-digit number.

79 twos = 80 twos − 1 two

        79 x 2 =

198 threes = 200 threes − 2 threes

        198 x 3 =

➢ Multiplying by 5. 2 fives = 10. Multiply by 10, then half the product.

        26 x 5 =

Division

➤ Divide a number by 2.

Half of 38 = half of 40 − half of 2.

$$38 \div 2 =$$

Half of 116 = half of 120 − half of 4.

$$116 \div 2 =$$

➤ Divide a number by 5.

$90 \div 5 =$ double 90 ÷ double 5.

$$90 \div 5 =$$

$320 \div 5 =$ double 320 ÷ double 5.

$$320 \div 5 =$$

Lesson
Planning

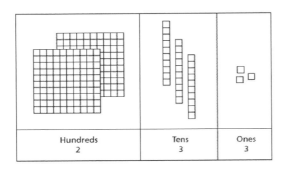

hundreds	tens	ones
100 100	10 10 10	1 1 1

Singapore Math Lesson Components

1. Mental Math
2. Teacher Directed: concrete, pictorial, abstract
3. Guided Practice: concrete, pictorial, abstract
4. Activity
5. Independent Practice
6. Home enjoyment!

Assessment with Singapore Math

Primary Mathematics materials include:

- Textbooks that provide practice for each topic that may be used as formative assessment. At the end of the unit, a comprehensive review of each topic is provided.
- Workbooks offer practice exercises with each topic, as well as topical and comprehensive reviews.
- Tests books provide multiple choice and open-ended styles of assessments for each topic as well as cumulative tests.
- Teacher's Guides include challenges and activities and instruct the teacher how to utilize materials contained within the lesson to assess students' learning.
- Supplemental materials to provide challenge or extra practice. A full listing of materials available begins on page 89.
- Placement tests that allow teachers to identify weaknesses and gaps in student content knowledge are available at singaporemath.com. These should not be sent home, but rather used to guide instruction in a classroom.

Types of Assessment and Their Purposes

Pre-assessment (also called entry-level)
- Do students have prerequisite skills/knowledge?
- Do students already know some of the upcoming material?

Formative (or progress monitoring)
- Fosters development and improvement **within** an activity.
- Guides instruction

Summative
- Assesses whether results meet stated goals or objectives.

Home Enjoyment as Formative Assessment

Checking each student's class work and home enjoyment is an obvious way to monitor progress.

If home enjoyment is important enough to assign, it's important enough for a teacher to check.

Students should be given feedback on homework as soon as possible and should correct their own mistakes as a means of learning. Through regular progress monitoring, a teacher can see if instruction needs to be repeated, clarified, approached in a different way, etc.

How Can Parents Help Their Child with Home Enjoyment?

Dealing with parents is frequently a challenge when Singapore Math is newly introduced. Generally speaking, parents did not learn math the way it is taught in Singapore and they do not understand the curriculum. The mental math strategies taught in first, second and third grade may be new to them, and bar modeling is almost inevitably something with which they are not familiar. Parents who are accustomed to helping their children with homework may not be able to do so by looking at the student workbook. In frustration, parents may simply tell their children, "Just do the problem this way," and teach the algorithm they learned in school, thereby defeating the Singaporean process of having the student understand the "why" math works prior to being taught "how" to solve the problem.

In addition, once students are in third grade, there is review work that will have to be done from the second grade Singapore Math materials in order to create the strong foundation for continued mathematical success. Third grade students are sometimes frustrated by the new curriculum because they "don't get it."

What can parents do? Help with the mastery of basic math facts. By the time a student completes third grade, Singapore Math curriculum expects that student to have mastered addition and subtraction within 100 mentally, and all multiplication/division facts through their 10's tables. In order for this to happen, parents are going to have to help.

Flashcards, computer websites, having the child figure out the total of a few items at the grocery store, or the change due back upon payment, goes a long way. Even super-busy parents can spend a few minutes a day (at the dinner table or in the car, if need be), quizzing their child on their multiplication facts.

In addition to working math facts, parents can also:

- Encourage and allow their child to count change.
- Help their child tell time on an analog clock.
- Work with their child with measurement: cooking, carpentry, travel etc.

Parents:

- ✓ May see <u>home enjoyment</u> with fewer but more challenging problems.
- ✓ Need to allow their child to work math using <u>Singapore Math methods.</u>

Students:

- ✓ Are expected to practice <u>math facts</u> daily.

Some Suggestions on Introducing Parents to Singapore Math Methods

1. Explain why you're incorporating Singapore Math into the classroom.

2. Explain Singapore Math. (Think "Singapore Math in a nutshell".)

3. Inform parents about the training you have already completed!

4. Show/explain the materials. They are different than what parents are used to.

5. Tell the parents your home enjoyment policy. At this time you can explain what type of work the parents **can** be doing with their children at home.

    a. Math Facts: Not just multiplication!

    b. Mental Math: You will need to go over in more detail. Explain how it is used in your class and give several examples of what parents can do with their children.

6. Inform the parents of the key topics that will be covered in your grade level.

7. Prepare for different objections:

    a. "Why can't I help my child the way I learned/know?"

    b. "What happens after my child leaves this curriculum?"

8. Demonstrate some components:

    a. Number Bonds

    b. Decomposing

    c. Model Drawing

Problem Solving

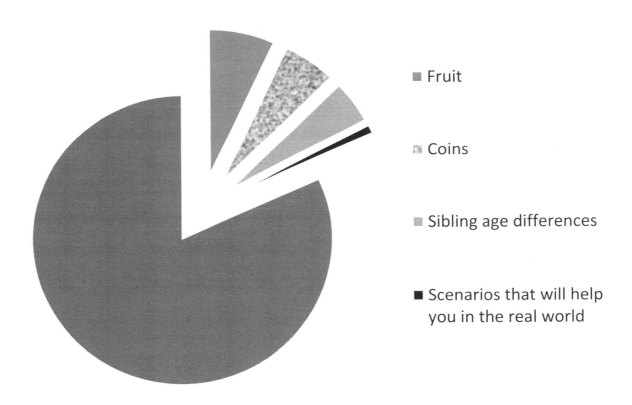

- Fruit
- Coins
- Sibling age differences
- Scenarios that will help you in the real world

Problem Solving with Singapore Math

"There are two aims which the teacher may have in view when addressing to his students a question or a suggestion... First, to help the student to solve the problem at hand. Second, to develop the student's ability so that he may solve future problems by himself."
    - George Polya

What is a Problem?

A problem is a task for which:

✓ The person confronting it wants or needs to find a solution.

✓ The person has no readily available procedure for finding the solution.

✓ The person must make an attempt to find a solution.

Charles and Lester. *Problem solving: What, why and how?* (1984).

"Problem solving should be the central focus of the mathematics curriculum... Problem solving is not a distinct topic but a process that should permeate the entire program and provide the context in which concepts and skills can be learned."

-Principles and standards for school mathematics, NCTM, 1989 p. 23

Why Teach Problem Solving Skills?

1. Help students deal with problems creatively and effectively
2. Stimulate pupils and help develop thinking skills and problem-solving strategies in both new and unfamiliar situations
3. Develop, reinforce, enhance and extend mathematical concepts and skills in pupils
4. Develop a sense of inquiry in pupils
5. Help pupils engage in imaginative and creative work arising from mathematical ideas

Steps in Problem Solving

1. **See** – Understanding the problem.
   - What information is given?
   - What can I identify?
   - Can I visualize the information?
   - Can I restate the problem without numbers?
   - How can I organize the information

2. **Plan** – Devising a plan.
   - What operation should I use, how do I solve this?
   - Have I seen a similar problem before?

3. **Do** – Carry out the plan.
   - Take your time!
   - Do I need to revise or modify the plan?
   - Am I using computational skills and logical reasoning?

4. **Look Back** - Reflect!
   - Does my answer satisfy the question?
   - Does it make sense?
   - Have I shown my work?
   - Is there another way to solve the problem? A simpler way?

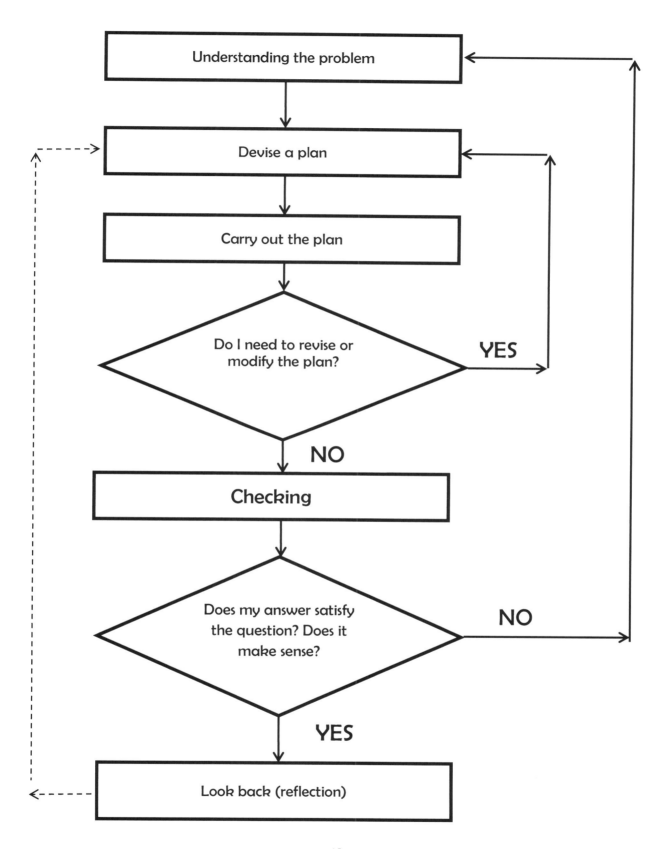

41

Adapted from Shaping Maths, 3a Teacher's Resource Pack

1. Reading & Understanding
    - o   Do you know the meaning of the words in the question?
    - o   What information is given?
    - o   What do you want to find?

2. Planning & Doing
    - o   What do you want to find first? How?
    - o   What do you want to find next? How?

    How?
    - o   *Do you need to find a part or the whole?*
    - o   *Do you need to find the difference or one of the sets?*
    - o   *Do you need to find how many times, how many equal groups or how many in a group?*

3. Checking
    - o   What have you done to solve the problem?
    - o   Have you added/subtracted/multiplied/divided correctly?
    - o   Read the question again. Does your answer make sense?
    - o   Estimate and check you solution.

Problem Solving Heuristics

Heuristics serve different purposes such as helping students to:

- understand the problem;
- simplify the task;
- identify possible causes;
- identify possible solutions;
- think or reason.

They are often used in combinations to solve the problem.

A brief description of the eleven heuristics suggested by the Singapore Ministry of Education is listed below.

1. Act it out

Take on the role of people, things or process in the problem and try to do what they do. It may sometimes be helpful to make use of objects to represent the situation or problem.

2. Make a systematic list

Organize the data such as numbers or type of objects logically into tables or lists. This helps the child identify and spot missing data asked for in the problem. Organized tabulation of data also helps the child perceive trends or patterns in the data.

3. Look for pattern(s)

Examine the available data for patterns or relationships. Having perceived a pattern, the child can then predict the missing data or answer.

4. Work backwards

Look at the end results and work backwards towards the beginning. This strategy can be useful in problems involving a series of steps or computations. It is also useful when the problem gives more data about the end condition and little data about its beginning.

5. Use before after concept

Compare the situation before and after the problem is solved. Sometimes the differences (or a specific difference) can shed light on the cause and lead to a possible solution.

6. Use guess and check

Make an educated guess of the answer and check to see if it is correct. Use the knowledge gained from testing an incorrect guess to improve the next guess. It is important to avoid making wild guesses. Track the guesses made and look for patterns to improve the next guess.

7. Make suppositions

Study the data given and make suppositions (assumptions without proof) about some aspects of the problem to form the basis for further thinking. This reduces the number of possibilities and makes it easier to explore the problem further.

8. Restate the problem in another way

Read the problem carefully and restate it in the child's own words. This helps the child understand the problem and identify important factors of the problem.

9. Simplify the problem

Make a difficult problem simpler. This can be done by changing complex numbers to simple numbers or by reducing the number of things in the problem. The solution to the simplified problem may help the child solve the original problem.

10. Solve part of the problem

Split a complex problem into smaller parts and solve the simpler part first.

11. Use a diagram / model

Draw a diagram / model to create a pictorial description of the problem. This helps the child to visualize and understand the problem. Drawing also enables the child to "manipulate" the data.

Sample Problems

Act it out

Arrange 6 discs in the shape below. Move only 2 discs to form a circle.

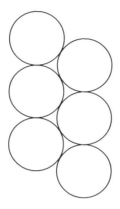

Make a systematic list

Ben has 13 coins totaling $1.20 in his pocket. He has a combination of quarters, dimes and nickels. How many of each coin does he have?

Quarters	Dimes	Nickels	Number of coins	Amount of money
4	2	0	6	$1.20
2	5	4	11	$1.20
2	4	6	12	$1.20

Look for patterns

$$\square + \bigcirc = 19$$
$$\bigcirc + \triangle = 26$$
$$\square + \triangle = 11$$

$$\square + \bigcirc + \triangle = ?$$

Work backwards

At the store Sam bought baseball cards for $1.35, he then spent 75 cents on the bus. Sam had $2.37 left over. How much money did he begin with?

Guess and Check

In an open book, the product of two facing page numbers is 6. Could the product of two facing page numbers be 240 in this book? Give the reason for your answer.

Simplify the problem

When the first 100 whole numbers are added up, what is the total?

Draw a picture or diagram

We have pigs and chickens in our barnyard. I count 7 heads and 20 feet. How many pigs and how many chickens are out there?

A supermarket is open from 10:15 am to 6:30 pm every day. How long is the supermarket open each day?

A night tour began at 10:30pm and lasted 3 hours 20 minutes.
When did the night tour end?

Why Model Drawing?

What makes model drawing so effective is less about the specific model—the rectangles—than the systematic and consistent way it is taught. Each grade level addresses distinct operations and number relationships—addition and subtraction in second grade, multiplication and division in third, fractions and ratios in fourth and fifth—so students can visualize and solve increasingly complex problems.

- Problem Solving In Singapore Math, Andy Clark

It's true; there is no single "best way" for solving word problems. No wonder students find them challenging! Working through word problems, however, is how students realize the importance of and applications of mathematics. One key benefit of the Model Drawing method is that students have a strategy that works for many types of word problems: addition, subtraction, multiplication, division, fractions, ratio and percentage. It provides students with a visual understanding of a problem that they can translate into a diagram, then the arithmetic necessary to find a solution.

As Andy Clark states above, the drawing is not so rigid as to need to be done in a certain way or with particular steps. Rather, the drawing of a model can be boiled down to:

- Understand the problem
- Translate the problem into a diagram
- Do the arithmetic

Typically, rectangles are used because they are easy to draw and will work for most situations.

Beginning students can use centimeter graph paper or even turn their lined paper sideways to draw unit bars that are proportional in length.

Furthermore, although students love to draw brackets, they can be challenging.

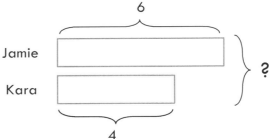

This handbook will make use of several variations.

Jamie has 6 apples. Kara has 4 apples. How many apples do they have altogether?

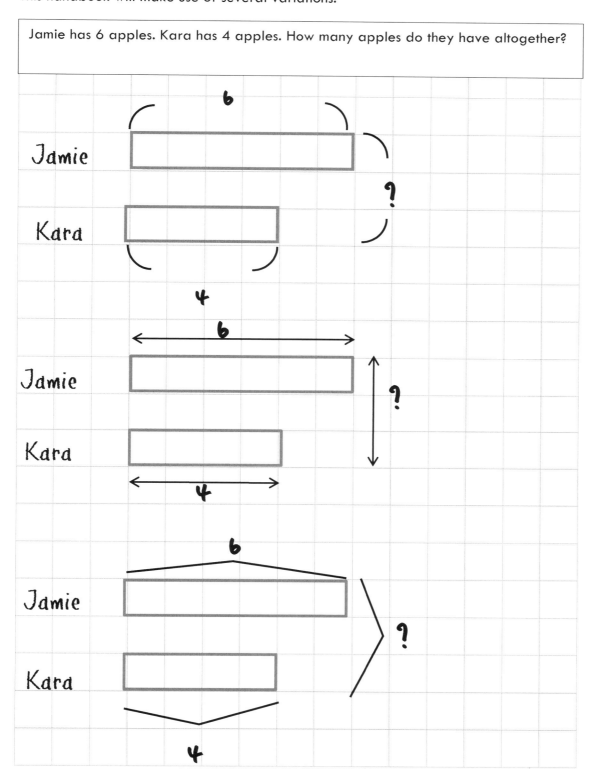

Stages of model- drawing

Jamie has 4 apples. Kara has 1 apple. How many apples do Jamie and Kara have altogether?

1. Pictorial representation

For emergent readers, images of students can be used instead of names.

2. Concrete Representation

Use Cuisenaire Rods, Unifix Cubes, Snap Cubes, etc...

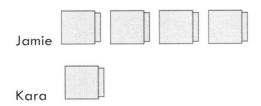

3. Pictorial Representation

Model drawing progresses from less to more abstract.

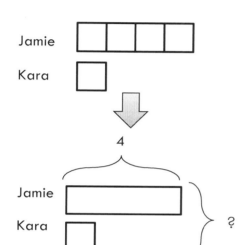

A final solution might look like:

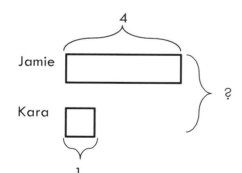

$4 + 1 = 5$

Jamie and Kara have 5 apples altogether.

Part – Whole Models

In this model, the two quantities are considered the parts of the whole. The model provides a visual representation of the part-whole (or part-part-whole) relationship. Either part or the whole could be the unknown quantity.

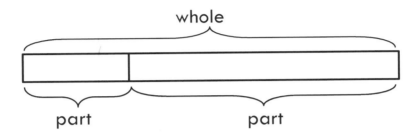

whole

part   part

Donna has 3 books. Her friend gave her 2 more. How many books does Donna have altogether?

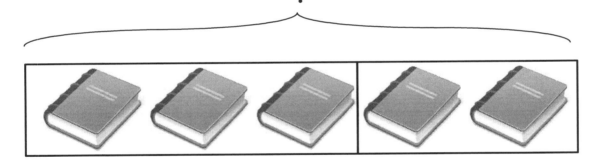

Donna has 5 books. She has 2 spelling books and the rest are math books. How many math books does Donna have?

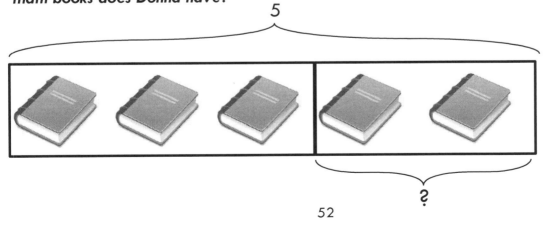

Comparison Models

Amy has 3 more apples than bananas. If Amy has 8 apples, how many bananas does she have?

In the **first grade**, students use concrete manipulatives to match or compare the quantities of apples and bananas:

There are 8 apples. There are 3 more apples than bananas.

In the **second grade**, students will use a pictorial model:

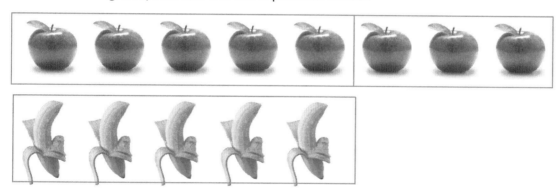

Grade 3 students will progress to the more abstract comparison model.

This model provides a visual representation of the relationships between the three quantities.

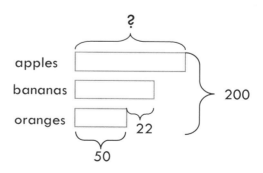

Multiplication and Division

Part-Whole Models:

Each chair has 4 legs. How many legs do 6 chairs have altogether?

In the second grade, students begin with concrete representations when discussing equal groups.

In the third grade and beyond, students will use a pictorial model that is more abstract. The part-whole relationship consists of equal parts.

whole or multiples of one unit

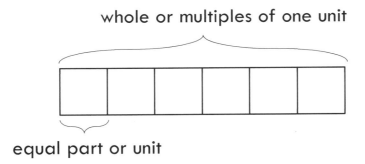

equal part or unit

Comparison Models

There are 4 chairs. There are 3 times as many tables as chairs. How many tables are there?

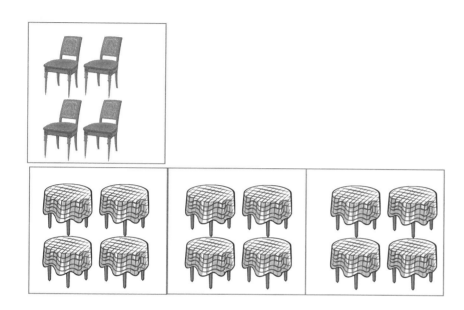

The pictorial representation is introduced in second and third grade, and then progresses to the more abstract model in third grade. The comparison model for multiplication and division provides a visual representation of the relationships between the three quantities.

larger quantity

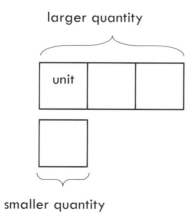

smaller quantity

Multi-Step Problems

Multi-step problems combine 2 different operations - the most interesting cannot be classified as a +, - , x, or ÷ problem.

Sam had 366 stamps in his collection. He had 98 fewer stamps than Thomas. How many stamps do they have altogether?

How can a student restate the question without numbers to show that they have understood the problem?

> Example: "Sam had some stamps. He had less than Thomas. The question is asking how many stamps they had if they put their collections together."

Next, draw a representative model. Since we know that Sam has fewer stamps than Thomas, his bar should be shorter. This is a good point to work on estimation. How much longer should Thomas' bar be than Sam's bar?

Sam

Thomas

Now add the information that is given in the problem:

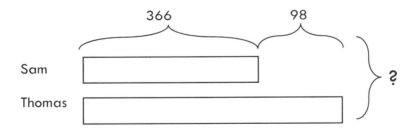

It's easy to see from our model that we're missing some information. Before we can add Sam and Thomas' stamps together, we need to find out how many stamps Thomas has. That's a simple equation!

366 + 98 = 464 stamps.   **Thomas has 464 stamps.**

That information can be added to the model:

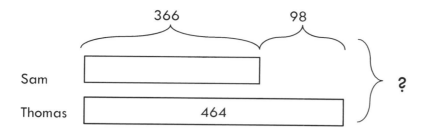

All that is left is a simple computation and a sentence:

```
  464
+ 366
  830
```

They had 830 stamps altogether.

* Note: It is perfectly possible to solve this problem in a single step without finding the number of Thomas' stamps by adding: 366 + 366 + 98.

Keep it organized!

Part of the challenge of multi-step problems is keeping the work organized. When introducing bar model drawing, you may want students to begin by organizing their workspace. Be sure to give students plenty of space to work! One way to introduce two step problems is to have students divide their workspace in half and list the steps individually. Students may begin by drawing a separate model for each step.

Sam had 366 stamps in his collection. He had 98 fewer stamps than Thomas. How many stamps do they have altogether?

Step 1: Find how many stamps Thomas had.

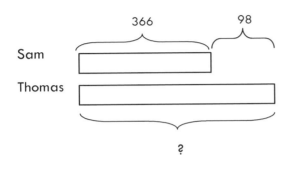

$366 + 98 = 464$ stamps.

Thomas has 464 stamps.

Step 2: Find how many stamps altogether.

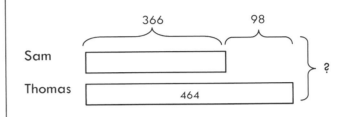

$$\begin{array}{r} 366 \\ +\ 464 \\ \hline 830 \end{array}$$

They had 830 stamps altogether.

The next problem was written by a third-grade student.

> *Natasha and Analisa have 384 meatballs altogether. Natasha has five times as many meatballs as Analisa. How many does each girl get?*

1. The student begins by dividing the number of meatballs by the total units, 6. She finds that each unit box has a value of 64 meatballs.

2. Unsure as to the next step, the student begins to divide the value of each unit box by 6, and then realizes that's not quite right.

3. The student then multiplies the unit value (64) by the total number of units for Natasha and finds the number of meatballs Natasha has.

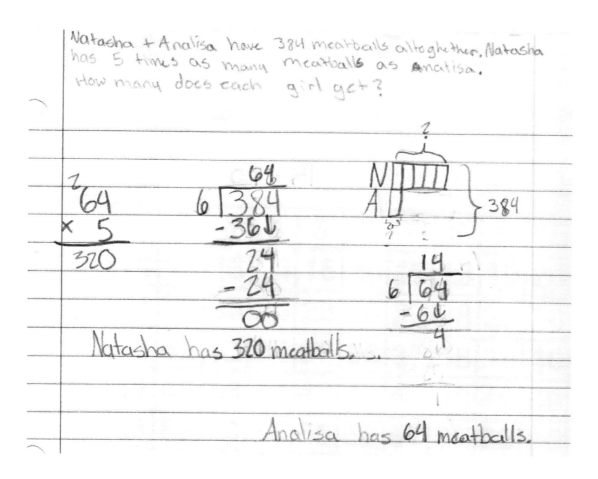

Natasha + Analisa have 384 meatballs altogether. Natasha has 5 times as many meatballs as Analisa. How many does each girl get?

Natasha has 320 meatballs.

Analisa has 64 meatballs.

This problem is also from third-grade:

Margo has three times as many pears as apples. If she has 84 pears and apples altogether, how many pears does she have?

She has 63 pears.

1. The student begins by dividing the number of pears and apples into four equal groups.
2. The student then multiplies the unit value (21) by the total number of units of pears.

Different ways of solving a problem

"Being able to and tending to solve a problem in more than one way, therefore, reveals the ability and the predilection to make connections between and among mathematical areas and topics"   -Liping Ma

The difference between two numbers is 3146. If the bigger number is 3 times the smaller number, find the sum of the two numbers.

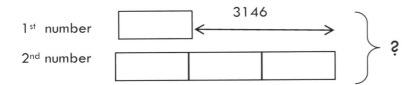

Once students get to this point, their model may show them several different computation strategies.

1. Solve for one unit, then find each number.
   Add each number together to get the sum.

$3146 \div 2 = 1573$

$1573 \times 3 = 4719$

$4719 + 1573 = \textbf{6292}$

2. Solve for one unit then multiply by 4

$3146 \div 2 = 1573$

$1573 \times 4 = \textbf{6292}$

3. Since there are 4 equal units and the total value of two of them is already known, double that.

$3146 \times 2 = \textbf{6292}$

Any way you get there, the answer is: **The sum of the numbers is 6292.**

Elapsed Time

Consider elapsed time linearly, as on a timeline:

Minnie watched a TV program that started at 8:30am and ended at 10:15 am. How long did the program last?

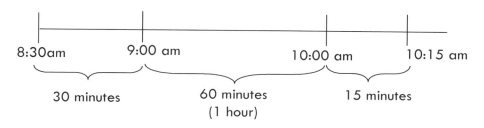

30 min+60 min+15 min = 75 min   **The program lasted 1 hour 45 minutes.**

Mr. Evans works from 9:30am to 6:15pm. His lunch break is from 1:00 pm to 2 pm and his coffee break is from 3:15pm to 3:30pm. How many hours does Mr. Evans work in a day?

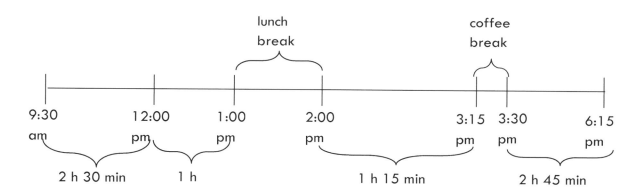

2 h 30 min
1 h
1 h 15 min
<u>2 h 45 min</u>
6 h 90 min or 7 hrs 30 mins

Mr. Evans works 7 hours and 30 minutes in a day.

Fractions

Bar models can help students visualize complex fraction concepts. Many word problems use round pieces of food: cookies, pizza, cake, pies, etc. A bar model provides a more transferable visual for fractions.

Ian ate $\frac{2}{6}$ of a pizza and Lisa at $\frac{3}{6}$ of it. What fraction of the pizza did the children eat?

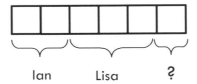

Ian   Lisa   ?

$\frac{2}{6} + \frac{3}{6} = \frac{5}{6}$ **The students ate $\frac{5}{6}$ of the pizza.**

Liz painted $\frac{1}{5}$ of signpost red and $\frac{1}{4}$ of the remainder blue. The rest of the signpost was white. What fraction of the signpost was white?

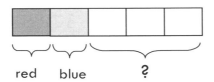

red   blue   ?

If the part of the signpost painted red was 2 feet long, how long was the part that was white?

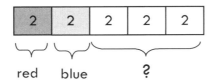

red   blue   ?

red   → 1 ☐ = 2 feet

white → 3 ☐ = 3 x 2 feet = 6 feet

62

Before and After Models

A change scenario can require a more complex bar model. Change problems are written as a *before* and *after* situation:

Julio had 64 comic books. He gave 19 to his little brother. How many comic books did Julio have left?

<u>Before</u>

number of comic books

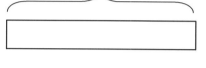

<u>After</u>

number of comic books

$64 - 19 = 45$ **Julio had 45 comic books left.**

Tara spent $\frac{1}{4}$ of her money at the bookstore. She spent $\frac{1}{3}$ of the money she had left at bowling alley. Altogether, Tara spent $36. How much money did she have at first?

<u>Before</u>

amount of money

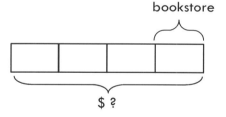

<u>After</u>

amount of money

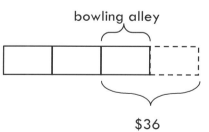

2 ☐ → $36
1 ☐ → $36 ÷ 2 = $18
3 ☐ → $18 x 4 = $72

Tara had $72 at first.

After Ryan gave 128 stickers to Lenny, they had the same number of stickers. If they had 448 stickers altogether, how many stickers did Ryan have at first?

For this problem, it's best to **begin at the end.** A dotted line or unit can represent a shift or movement of a bar:

After

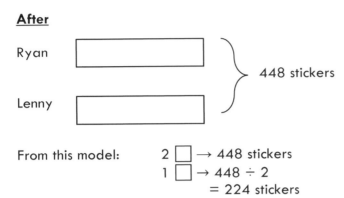

From this model:

$2 \square \rightarrow 448$ stickers
$1 \square \rightarrow 448 \div 2$
$= 224$ stickers

They each had 224 stickers at the end. Since the question asks, "How many did Ryan have at first?" we can put what we know into a *before* model:

Before

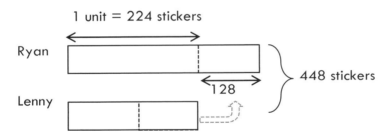

The number of stickers Ryan had at first $\rightarrow 224 + 128$
$= 352$ stickers.

Ryan had 352 stickers at first.

64

Percentage Problems

Both a bar model and a percentage ruler can be used to create a model of a percentage problem.

A class of 40 students chose their favorite candy. 25% of the students chose licorice, 15% chose lollipops and the rest chose chocolate. How many students chose chocolate as their favorite candy?

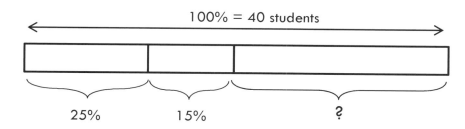

100% = 40 students

25%   15%   ?

100- 25 – 15 = 60%

60% x 40 = 24 students   **24 students chose chocolate.**

Travis bought a skateboard that cost $60. Andy spent 20% more on his skateboard. How much did Andy spend on his skateboard?

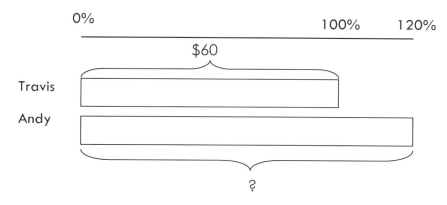

0%   100%   120%

$60

Travis

Andy

?

Andy spent 120% of what Travis spent.

Method #1

100% → $60

1% → $0.6

120% → 120 x .6 = $72

Method #2

120% of $60 = $\frac{120}{100}$ x $60

Andy spent $72

Ratio

A ratio is a comparison of any two (or multiple) quantities. The concept of proportion is closely linked with ratio.

The ratio of the number of red and blue cars is 4 : 5. If there are 30 blue cars, how many red cars are there?

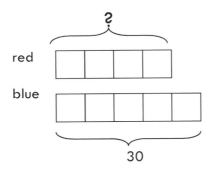

$5 \,\square \rightarrow 30$

$1 \,\square \rightarrow 30 \div 5 = 6$

$4 \,\square \rightarrow 4 \times 6 = 24$

There are 24 red cars.

Ramli and Tim had the same amount of money at first. After Ramli spent $10 and Tim spent $6.50, the ratio of Ramli's money to Tim's money was 3 : 4. How much money did they each have at first?

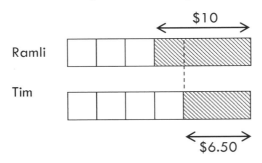

Ramli began with 3 units and $10

Tim began with 4 units and $6.50

$1 \,\square \rightarrow \$10 - \$6.50 = \$3.50$

$4 \,\square \rightarrow 4 \times \$3.50 = \$14$

$\$14 + \$6.50 = \$20.50$

They each had $20.50 at first.

Assessing Word Problems

When assessing word problems, the solution method is a significant part of the answer. Students should expect to show their work to get full credit for a problem. A word problem might consist of points for the method of solving as well as points for correct computation and answers.

Let's go back to meatball problem:

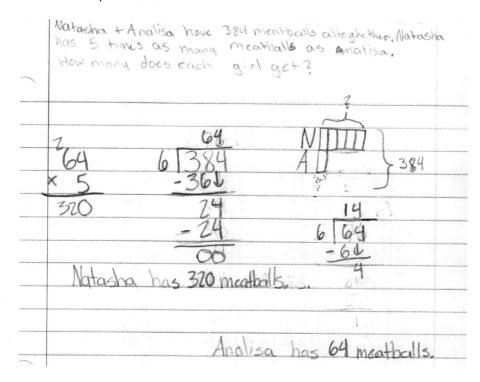

This was part of an introduction to two-step problems. It was worth five points:

- 1 point for a representative diagram
- 1 point for correct labeling, including the "?" to represent what is unknown.
- 1 point for computation on the first step
- 1 point for computation on the second step
- 1 point for a correct answer in a complete sentence

As students progress, the rubric may change. At the end of a unit/school year, the same problem might be worth three points; one apiece for diagram, computation, solution.

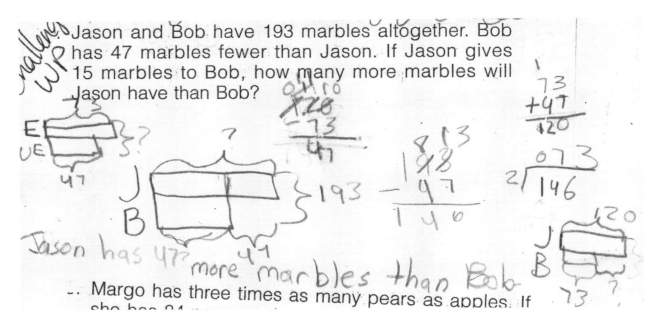

Jason and Bob have 193 marbles altogether. Bob has 47 marbles fewer than Jason. If Jason gives 15 marbles to Bob, how many more marbles will Jason have than Bob?

Margo has three times as many pears as apples. If she has 24

This student started correctly:

- ✓ The bar model for J & B is perfect.
- ✓ He subtracts 47 from 193 to find the value of the two units-146.
- ✓ He divides 146 by two to find that Bob has 73 marbles.
- ✓ He adds 73 and 47 to find that Jason has 120 marbles.

Then down in the bottom right corner of the workspace, the student compares Jasons' current quantity of marbles to Bob's current amount, missing the change part of the question where Jason gives 15 marbles to Bob.

This was a problem for a gifted third grade student that was assigned as home enjoyment. As such, it would be worth 5 points and the student's work would earn:

2 points for a representative diagram and correct labeling
1 point for computation

We would work this problem together the next day. Note that there should have been a lot more working space for this problem.

This same problem on an end of year assessment would be work 4 points and this student's score might be 1 out of 4:

$\frac{1}{2}$ point for the diagram and labeling and $\frac{1}{2}$ point for the computation.

68

Practice Problems

1. The total length of 2 pieces of rope is 18 yd. One piece of rope is 3 yd long. What is the length of the other piece of rope?

The length of the other piece of rope is _____ yd.

2. Four children bought a present for $28. They shared the cost equally. How much did each child pay?

3. Kendra made 280 egg salad sandwiches for a party. She made 3 times as many chicken sandwiches as egg salad sandwiches.

   How many chicken sandwiches did she make?

4. Linda has 18 dolls.
   (a) If she puts them on 2 shelves equally, how many dolls does she put on each shelf?

   (b) If she puts them on 3 shelves equally, how many dolls does she put on each shelf?

5. A fruit seller had 1136 oranges. 16 of them were rotten. He packed the rest into boxes of 8. How many boxes of oranges were there?

6. Aaron and Ben have 825 Pokémon cards altogether. If Aaron has 79 Pokémon cards less than Ben, how many Pokémon cards does Ben have?

7. Matt bought 5 times as many apples as Cecelia. Wilson bought 125 apples more than Cecelia. The three children had 1000 apples in all. How many apples did Wilson buy?

8. The difference between two numbers is 2,184. If the bigger number is 3 times the smaller number, find the sum of the two numbers.

9. After Jolene had given 128 stickers to Lynn, they had the same number of stickers. If they had 448 stickers altogether, how many stickers did Jolene have at first?

10. There were 48 chocolates in a box. After eating some of them, Tara found that she had $\frac{5}{8}$ of the chocolates left. How many chocolates did she eat?

11. Steve bought 2 bottles of orange juice and a bottle of apple juice for $6.55. The bottle of apple juice cost $0.35 less than the bottle of orange juice. What was the cost of one bottle of orange juice?

12. Tyrone bought a bag of marbles. $\frac{1}{4}$ of the marbles were blue, $\frac{1}{8}$ were green, and $\frac{1}{5}$ of the remainder were yellow. If there were 24 yellow marbles, how many marbles did he buy?

13. William had $500. He spent 24% of his money on transport and 36% on food.

(a) What percentage of his money was left?

(b) How much money was left?

14. Ian has $56. Brandon has 20% more money than Ian. How much money does Brandon have?

15. The ratio of the number of Jimmy's marbles to the number of Kelvin's marbles was 3:4. After Jimmy bought another 60 marbles, he had twice as many marbles as Kelvin. How many marbles did Jimmy have at first?

16. The average weight of Henry, Peter and John is 35.5 kg. Peter is twice as heavy as John. Henry is 4kg lighter than Peter. Find Peter's weight.

17. From the ACT COMPASS Math Placement exam

At Big Al's restaurant, three cheeseburgers and two orders of fries cost $5.60. Four cheeseburgers and three orders of fries cost $7.80.

How much does a single cheeseburger and a single order of fries each cost separately?

Resources

MATH DAYS

Celebrate mathematical holidays with this handy list!

Symbol	Value	Day
π	3.14159...	March 14 (any year)
e	2.71828...	February 7, 1828
ϕ	1.61803...	January 6, 1803
$\sqrt{23}$	4.79583...	April 7, 9:58am
i	$\sqrt{-1}$ (imaginary)	The day that people like math jokes

Miracle Math   by Barry Garelick

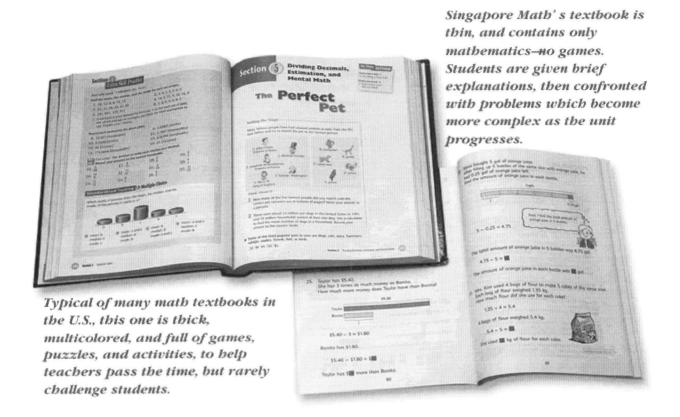

Singapore Math's textbook is thin, and contains only mathematics—no games. Students are given brief explanations, then confronted with problems which become more complex as the unit progresses.

Typical of many math textbooks in the U.S., this one is thick, multicolored, and full of games, puzzles, and activities, to help teachers pass the time, but rarely challenge students.

It was another body blow to education. In December of 2004, media outlets across the country were abuzz with news of the just-released results of the latest Trends in International Mathematics and Science Study (TIMSS) tests. Once again despite highly publicized efforts to reform American math education (some might say because of the reform efforts) over the past two decades, the United States did little better than average (see Figure 1). Headquartered at the International Study Center at Boston College and taken by tens of thousands of students in more than three dozen countries, TIMSS has become a respected standard of international academic achievement. And in three consecutive TIMSS test rounds (in 1995, 1999, and 2003), 4th- and 8th-grade students in the former British trading colony of Singapore beat all contenders, including math powerhouses Japan and Taiwan. United States 8th graders did not even make the top ten in the 2003 round; they ranked 16th. Worse, scores for American students were, as one Department of Education study put it, "among the lowest of all industrialized countries."

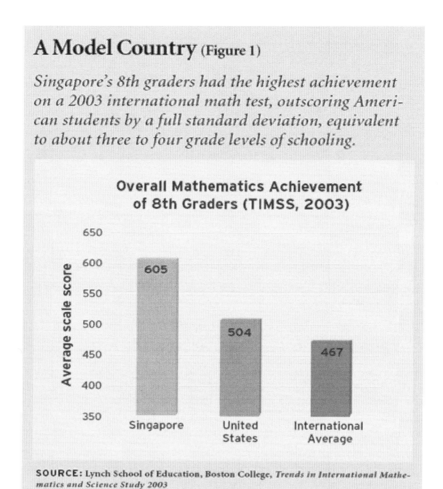

A Model Country (Figure 1)

Singapore's 8th graders had the highest achievement on a 2003 international math test, outscoring American students by a full standard deviation, equivalent to about three to four grade levels of schooling.

Overall Mathematics Achievement of 8th Graders (TIMSS, 2003)

Average scale score

Singapore	605
United States	504
International Average	467

SOURCE: Lynch School of Education, Boston College, *Trends in International Mathematics and Science Study 2003*

During the clamor over the TIMSS results (released in December 2004), I heard Robyn Silbey, a math "content coach" from a Rockville, Maryland, public school, being interviewed by Ira Flatow for his Science Friday program on National Public Radio. Silbey worked at College Gardens Elementary. She explained that her school was one of four in the Montgomery County Public Schools (MCPS) district experimenting with Singapore's math program. And, according to Silbey, it was working. The Singapore texts and methods were so effective in College Gardens that the scores of students there on the math computation portion of the standardized Comprehensive Tests of Basic Skills (CTBS) rose from the 50th and 60th percentiles to the low 90s in the first 4 years they were used.

I later learned that an evaluation of the pilot program conducted by MCPS found that in the schools where Singapore Math (SM) was being used as a pilot program, students typically outperformed their peers in other district schools. Yet despite these positive results, three of the four pilot schools dropped out of the program after fewer than four years. Why, I wondered. If the county's own evaluation found benefits from Singapore Math, why not continue using it? In view of America's disappointing rankings in math and Singapore's record of success, why wasn't the Singapore Math program given a serious and extended try?

In the Beginning

While the story of Singapore Math in Montgomery County does not answer all the questions about the persistently poor math literacy of American students, the failure of the program to take hold there does provide disturbing clues about some of the institutional and governmental practices that impede improvement in education—and not just in Montgomery County.

In my early research into what happened in Montgomery County, I met John Hoven, then co-president of the Gifted and Talented Association of Montgomery County and now a national advisor to NYC HOLD (New York City Honest Open Logical Decisions on Mathematics Education Reform), a nonpartisan advocacy organization that provides information to parents, teachers, and others on math education issues. Hoven, an economist in the Antitrust Division of the U.S. Department of Justice by day, had discovered Singapore Math while waging a successful battle to get MCPS to forgo a National Science Foundation (NSF) grant worth $6 million. The grant would have trained teachers to use a middle-school program called Connected Math, one of several, Hoven learned, that was funded by the Education and Human Resources Division of the NSF and based on standards developed by the National Council of Teachers of Mathematics (NCTM). Though the NCTM is a private organization, it exerts enormous influence over the math standards and texts used by most states and districts in the United States—standards and texts that, in Hoven's view, were failing.

During the campaign against the Connected Math grant, Hoven discovered Singapore Math. He learned that Singapore, whose population is half that of New York City, had begun modifying its education policies in the early 1980s to build up its labor force in such a way as to create technical skills unavailable elsewhere in the Third World. The Curriculum Development Institute of Singapore (now called the Curriculum Planning & Development Institute) had created the math program and the accompanying texts, called Primary Mathematics (which were published in English, Singapore's official administrative language, in 1982), to help boost that technological prowess. The Primary Mathematics series was at the heart of Singapore's national math curriculum as it achieved its successive TIMSS victories.

Many professional mathematicians, concerned with the decline of math education in the United States, took a hard look at the Singapore Math methods and texts and liked what they saw. The texts have been distributed in the United States by an Oregon company since 1998 and are used by many home-school parents and promoted by Internet-based parent and professional organizations. In addition, the private nonprofit Rosenbaum Foundation helped fund the implementation of Singapore Math programs in scattered sites around the United States and in Israel. A study of Singapore Math conducted by the American Institutes for Research (AIR) for the U.S. Department of Education (released in January 2005) concluded, "What the United States needs overall are the sound features of the Singapore Mathematics system." In studying several different American school districts that were experimenting with the program, including the Montgomery County Public Schools, AIR researchers found that "Singapore Mathematics textbooks can produce significant boosts in achievement." But the AIR report also cautioned that making Singapore Math work in the United States "will require the same sustained commitment to developing a quality mathematics system that Singapore gave to its reform efforts."

That was a lesson still to be learned in Maryland.

A Long Way from Singapore to Montgomery County

John Hoven and his allies persuaded the Montgomery County Public Schools to try Singapore Math instead of pursuing the Connected Math grant, but instead of receiving $6 million, the district would have to spend its own funds. And that wouldn't be $6 million. "The initial plan was for a $50,000 pilot spread out over two years," Hoven recalls. "It was $50,000 in a $1 billion budget. The money would pay for textbooks and nothing else—no teacher training, nothing." Hoven knew it was just a drop in the bucket for the district, but he was sure that the Asian math program would sell itself.

MCPS selected four middle-class, ethnically diverse, suburban schools—College Gardens in Rockville, Charles R. Drew and Highland View in Silver Spring, and Woodfield in Gaithersburg—to participate in the pilot. But few teachers at the schools realized how different Singapore's approach to math was from what they had been used to; it was nothing less than a total shock to the schools' systems.

Unlike many American math textbooks, such as Math Thematics, published by Houghton Mifflin, which are thick, multicolored, and multicultural, Singapore's books are thin and contain only mathematics. There are no graphics (other than occasional cartoons pertaining to the lesson at hand), no spreadsheet problems, and no problems asking students to use a calculator to find the mean number of dogs in a U.S. household. With SM, students are required to show their mathematical work, not explain in essays how they did the problems or how they felt about them. While a single lesson in a U.S. textbook might span two pages and take one class period to go through, a lesson in a Singapore textbook might use five to ten pages and take several days to complete. The Singapore texts contain no narrative explanation of how a procedure or concept works; instead, there are problems and questions accompanied by pictures that provide hints about what is going on. According to the AIR report, the Singapore program "provides rich problem sets that give students many and varied opportunities to apply the concepts they have learned."

Another key difference is the number of topics covered by Singapore's texts for a single grade. The AIR study frequently criticizes American math texts for being an inch deep and a mile wide, covering a great range of topics with little time spent on developing the material, including mastery of math facts. (One of the texts with which the AIR study compares Singapore's Primary Mathematics series is Everyday Mathematics, a program developed with NSF funding and used widely in Montgomery County.) The MCPS 1st-grade curriculum goals, for instance, contain a number of nonessential topics, such as sorting concrete objects (like Post-its with names of favorite pets on them) into categories, activities that take up instructional time which, critics of the MCPS curriculum argue, could be better spent laying the foundation for algebra in 8th grade.

Singapore's texts also present material in a logical sequence throughout the grades and expect mastery of the material before the move to the next level. In contrast, mainstream American math texts and curricula frequently rely on a "spiral" approach, in which topics are revisited and reviewed. The expectation of that approach is that not all students achieve mastery the first time around. One Ohio school teacher familiar with the spiral approach summed up much of the criticism of the method on an Internet math forum, saying, students "can't remember how to do it when [they] do return—or if they do remember it, it's now being taught in a different way."

The most important feature of Singapore's texts is an ingenious problem-solving strategy built into the curriculum. Word problems are for most students the most difficult part of any mathematics course. Singapore's texts help students tackle them through a technique called "bar modeling," in which students draw a diagram to help them solve the problem. Typically, in U.S. texts, students are taught to use a method called "Guess and Check"—trying combinations of numbers until the right numbers are found that satisfy the conditions of the problem—a method that many professional mathematicians consider inefficient (see sidebar). The bar-modeling technique not only provides a powerful method for solving problems, but also serves as a link to algebra. Symbolic representation of problems, the mainstay of algebra, emerges as a logical extension of the bar-modeling technique.

What Happened in Montgomery County?

Given all of the mathematical strengths of the Singapore program, why was the pilot abandoned so quickly in Montgomery County? The simplest answer is that where Singapore Math worked the best, in College Gardens, it is still being used; where it didn't work as well, it was dropped. But that does not begin to explain what happened.

All four Montgomery County schools used the Singapore Math texts in 2000–01 and 2001–02, but only College Gardens and Highland View kept the program in 2002–03. The "math computation" scores at College Gardens show a dramatic improvement for both 2nd and 4th grades (see Figures 2a and 2b), but in "general math" there is no discernible pattern; all four schools had either no change or a decrease in scores. Additional results from the pilot were detailed in the evaluation conducted by the MCPS Office of Shared Accountability after the second year of the experiment. The county evaluators found that students in the four Singapore Math pilot schools generally progressed through the curriculum at an accelerated pace compared with their peers in control schools.

But while the school district's evaluation was positive in tone (Singapore Math "helped prepare students for higher-level math placements in middle school"), it reported mixed results and offered no recommendation for expansion. Because the effectiveness of a program as sophisticated and multidimensional as Singapore Math cannot be thoroughly evaluated in just two years of testing, the story of its failure in Montgomery County says more about school politics and finances than about math programs. (It would help, for instance, to track students who went through Singapore's program through their 8th-grade tests to ascertain how well they were prepared for algebra.)

The mixed math results of the county's evaluation should have been seen for what they were: an interim assessment. Instead, the county ended the funding for the program after the second year. If schools wished to continue, they had to pay for the materials out of their own budgets, which they didn't need to do if they used district-approved texts such as Everyday Mathematics.

Detailing the many reasons for dropping support for the pilot by Montgomery County without waiting for long-term results would take more space than is available here. But we can get a sense of the thing by examining some of the reasons that the three schools gave for quitting Singapore Math and those given by College Gardens for staying with it.

The first problem was lack of planning and preparation. The depth and breadth of the differences between Singapore Math and American math were not appreciated. The decision to use Singapore Math was made in 1999, for instance, but textbooks and other teaching materials did not arrive at the four schools until late spring the following year, giving teachers just three months to prepare to introduce the program to students in the fall of 2000.

The Singapore Math manuals were another problem: they provided very little guidance on how to teach a particular lesson—because they are written for teachers who, for the most part, have a deeper understanding of mathematics than most U.S. teachers do. That dilemma was compounded by the lack of experience with Singapore's program by Montgomery County and its delay in training teachers to use it. The Montgomery County Public Schools eventually developed a training program, but some people believe it was too

Early Evidence (Figures 2a and 2b)

Two years after Singapore Math was introduced, 4th graders in the four Montgomery County (Maryland) schools implementing the program scored higher in math computation. However, the scores on the general mathematics section were flat or negative.

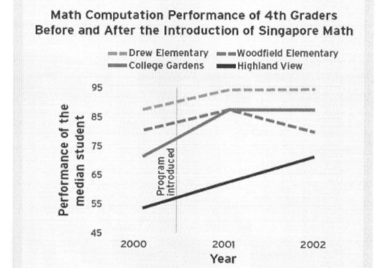

Math Computation Performance of 4th Graders Before and After the Introduction of Singapore Math

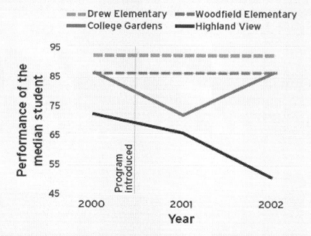

General Mathematics Performance of 4th Graders Before and After the Introduction of Singapore Math

Note: Performance is the national percentile rank on the Comprehensive Tests of Basic Skills (CTBS).

SOURCE: Maryland State Department of Education

84

little, too late. College Gardens and Highland View found funds to hire Singapore Math specialists (like Robyn Silbey) to help get the program off the ground and coordinate the training within their schools. Scott Baldridge, a Louisiana State University mathematician who provides professional training to teachers in implementing the Singapore program, believes that such training helps. "Some teachers get it on their own," he says, "but many need professional development to see how the curriculum interacts with the students over several years."

Even with adequate training, the two-year span of the pilot resulted in three of the pilot schools (all except College Gardens) introducing Singapore Math all at once, across all grades, which put older children at a severe disadvantage, since Singapore Math concepts build on one another. This helps to explain the difference in the math test results.

Another complaint expressed by teachers and administrators in all four schools was that Singapore Math was not in line with state standards. Indeed, the state's academic standards include data analysis, statistics, and probability, which Singapore's texts do not address. But it is more complicated than that since, by state law, each school district has authority over its own curriculum. Although required to administer the state tests, school districts are not required to align their curriculum with the state standards. That means, says Hoven, that "they can choose to aim for world-class standards instead, which at one time was one of the goals of the MCPS Long-Range Plan." But the plan was revised to be aligned with state standards instead—a move, say some, that was, in effect, a decision to lower Montgomery County's standards.

This brings us to the question of money. Eileen MacFarlane, principal at Drew, said that her school initially supplemented Singapore Math with additional material on statistics, data, and probability to cover the misalignment, but the cost of purchasing Singapore's materials from their own budget became a problem.

Joanne Steckler, now retired as principal of Highland View, said, "No one told us to drop the program." But being required to buy its own materials had the same effect. "For one year we did purchase our own Singapore materials," said Steckler. "But we did not want other curriculum areas to suffer because of lack of funds to purchase materials, so we gave up Singapore Math."

Shawn Miller, principal of Woodfield Elementary, also cited the cost of the texts. Once the county stopped funding Singapore Math, Miller made the decision to go with the county-approved program, Everyday Mathematics, which, he said, "was better aligned with the state curriculum."

With such standards-alignment and budget concerns, the schools had a safe way to bow out of the pilot.

A Culture Shock to the System

But budget questions were hardly fundamental. Taking on a program like Singapore Math meant going against what many teachers believed math education to be about; surely, it was not what they were trained for. Since the success of Singapore's programs relies in many ways on more traditional approaches to math education, such as explicit instruction and giving students many problems to solve, in some ways its very success represented a slap in the face to American math reformers, many of whom have worked hard to eliminate such techniques from the teaching canon.

Gail Burrill, a former president of the NCTM, suggests quite bluntly that the success of Singapore Math cannot be imported. "These are books used by a different culture, a culture that is more homogeneous, and a culture that has a consistent way of thinking about mathematics." And Cathy Seeley, a former president of the NCTM, hints as much by arguing that Singapore's success (as well as that of other Asian countries) is not about the textbook. "We have to look beyond their textbooks to determine what these lessons are."

The logic of the argument that it is the Asian culture or something "beyond their textbooks" that produces math success leads to the conclusion that, as NCTM adherents often contend, content doesn't matter nearly as much as the teacher or the culture that produces the "proper conditions for learning." Eileen MacFarlane maintained that the teachers in the Singapore pilots drew from the texts, but then quickly added, "The text is a resource, not a curriculum." She said this despite her enthusiasm for Singapore's program.

But the belief that the difference between Singapore Math and American math is just in the teaching or, as some suggest, the culture, is a rationalization, says David Klein, a mathematician at California State University, Northridge. "Math reformers assume that math education is bad in the United States because the NCTM reforms were not properly implemented nor understood by teachers," he continues. "They never consider the possibility that the NCTM standards themselves and the textbooks written for those standards are one of the causes of poor math education in this country."

The only person I heard openly disagree with the "teacher not text" argument was Dr. Sherry Liebes, then the principal of College Gardens, the only school that kept the program. While she said that teacher training is important, she added that Singapore's texts provide a structured curriculum, and thus "It's one less thing for teachers to worry about." This notion was echoed in the AIR study, which quoted a teacher in one of the pilot schools in Montgomery County: "Having to explain Singapore Mathematics made me understand that I never really understood the mathematics I was teaching."

Another stumbling block for the Maryland teachers was their concern that the Singapore Math program did not contain "real-world" activities. The term, as used by those who follow the ideas supported by the National Council of Teachers of Mathematics and education schools for teaching math, generally means a problem for which American students have not received much instruction or preparation. This is intentional, it turns out, because it is believed to be good for students to learn to approach problems for which they have not received explicit preparation. The National Education Association (NEA), for instance, in its online version of "A Parent's Guide to Helping Your Child with Today's Math," gives an example of a "real-world" problem:

A farmer sends his daughter and son out into the barnyard to count the number of chickens and pigs. When they return the son says that he counted 200 legs but the daughter says she counted 70 heads. How many pigs and chickens does the farmer have?

The NEA then suggests that some students may solve the problem using algebra (those who know how to do so, that is), while others might solve it using Guess and Check. Still others may choose to draw pictures to solve it. The NEA admits that some methods might be considered more efficient, but points out that the correct answer can be found using multiple methods and that "by allowing students to think flexibly about numbers, we encourage them to 'own' the math forever, instead of 'borrowing' until class is over." That this real-world problem depicts an approach that no sensible person would use in counting pigs and chickens is beside the point.

This kind of real-world math is indeed missing from Singapore's program—apparently, if TIMSS tests mean anything, without much harm. Rather than waste students' time with inefficient methods for solving problems, Singapore's texts provide instruction that eliminates trial and error, one of the goals of mathematics. Bar modeling is a powerful pictorial technique that results in one answer, deduced by using mathematical principles that students have learned rather than by employing the haphazard trial-and-error method of Guess and Check.

For One Brief Shining Moment

An exact description of which differences in math instruction matter most is perhaps impossible. For instance, an emphasis on sequential mastery of skills that builds on previously acquired skills is a key component of the Singapore Math program and not important in the American approach, where activities don't require such skills. While the latter creates the illusion of equal achievement, international tests like the TIMSS would seem to provide a reality check on that illusion.

The struggle to make math instruction work, of course, is not limited to Montgomery County. In the state of Washington, parent protests against the adoption of several standard math curricula (like Connected Math) led a state representative to introduce a bill earlier this year to put Singapore Math in all the state's elementary schools. And in New York City, Elizabeth Carson, who heads NYC HOLD, has led a battle for years to rid the city's schools of programs like Everyday Mathematics. She calls it a "tragedy for our children and our nation" that American attempts at math reform "bear no resemblance to the programs and standards of the highest-achieving nations."

Having watched as three of the four schools dropped Singapore's program in Montgomery County, John Hoven shared Carson's concern. Discouraged, he resigned a year ago from the county's Gifted and Talented Association. "I had stopped believing I could make a difference," he says. "I felt it was time for someone else to try."

In the meantime, the decline in the numbers of U.S.-trained scientists and engineers, compared with the increasing numbers of those trained in Asian countries, has not gone unnoticed. In this year's State of the Union address, President George W. Bush stated: "We need to encourage children to take more math and science, and make sure those courses are rigorous enough to compete with other nations." He proposed "to train 70,000 high-school teachers to lead Advanced Placement courses in math and science … bring 30,000 math and science professionals to teach in classrooms … and give early help to students who struggle with math, so they have a better chance at good, high-wage jobs."

A few months later, President Bush created the National Mathematics Advisory Panel to advise the White House and the secretary of education on the best use of scientifically based research to advance the teaching and learning of mathematics. The panel includes several people who have actively fought against the NCTM-led "fuzzy math" trend in this country.

While the goal of bolstering high-school math is a laudable one, the success of high-school students in math depends on what they've learned in the lower grades. If those foundations are weak, the addition of Advanced Placement courses in math and science in high schools will prove to be a weak enhancement. Unfortunately, changing the way math is taught in the lower grades appears to threaten an education philosophy and method that is pervasive in our schools, and does not move us towards academic excellence.

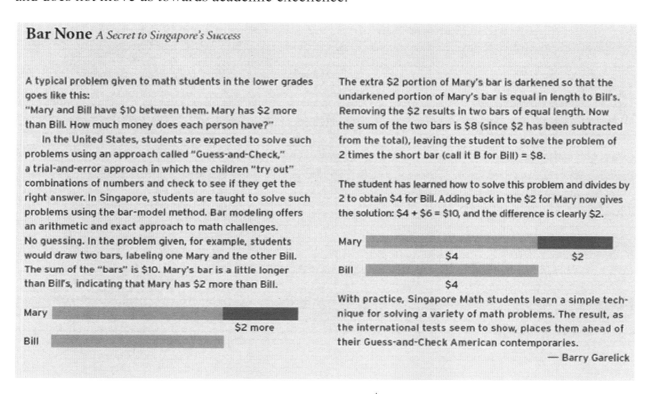

Bar None *A Secret to Singapore's Success*

A typical problem given to math students in the lower grades goes like this:

"Mary and Bill have $10 between them. Mary has $2 more than Bill. How much money does each person have?"

In the United States, students are expected to solve such problems using an approach called "Guess-and-Check," a trial-and-error approach in which the children "try out" combinations of numbers and check to see if they get the right answer. In Singapore, students are taught to solve such problems using the bar-model method. Bar modeling offers an arithmetic and exact approach to math challenges. No guessing. In the problem given, for example, students would draw two bars, labeling one Mary and the other Bill. The sum of the "bars" is $10. Mary's bar is a little longer than Bill's, indicating that Mary has $2 more than Bill.

Mary

$2 more

Bill

The extra $2 portion of Mary's bar is darkened so that the undarkened portion of Mary's bar is equal in length to Bill's. Removing the $2 results in two bars of equal length. Now the sum of the two bars is $8 (since $2 has been subtracted from the total), leaving the student to solve the problem of 2 times the short bar (call it B for Bill) = $8.

The student has learned how to solve this problem and divides by 2 to obtain $4 for Bill. Adding back in the $2 for Mary now gives the solution: $4 + $6 = $10, and the difference is clearly $2.

Mary

$4 $2

Bill

$4

With practice, Singapore Math students learn a simple technique for solving a variety of math problems. The result, as the international tests seem to show, places them ahead of their Guess-and-Check American contemporaries.

— Barry Garelick

This article is copyright © 2008 by the Board of Trustees of Leland Stanford Junior University and has been reproduced with permission. http://www.hoover.org/publications/ednext/3853357.html

REFERENCES:

Adler, S., Salerno, T. & Turner, C. (2009) *Singapore mental math meets core knowledge: Integrating mental math throughout the curriculum.* Available: www.singaporemathtraining.com

Aharoni, R. (2007). *Arithmetic for parents: A book for grownups about children's mathematics.* El Cerrito, CA: Sumizdat.

Baldridge, S. O. & Parker, T. A. (2007). *Elementary geometry for teachers.* Okemos, MI: Sefton-Ash Pub.

Baldridge, S. O. & Parker, T. A. (2004). *Elementary mathematics for teachers.* Okemos, MI: Sefton-Ash Pub.

Bronson, P., & Merryman, A. *New research: $13 Christmas gifts = 13 point gain in kids' IQ.* Newsweek. Dec. 10, 2009.

Er, A. (2007). *Mathematics Challenging Problems Primary 3.* Singapore: Educational Publishing House Pte Ltd. Available: www.eph.com.sg

Fanglan, L. (2007). *i-Excel: Heuristic and model approach, levels (1 – 6).* Singapore: Fan Learning Publications. Available: www.singaporemath.com

Fanglan, L. (2007). *MathExpress: Speed maths strategies, (levels 1 – 6).* Singapore: Fan Learning Publications. Available: www.singaporemath.com

Ginsburg, A., et. al. (2005). *What the United States can learn from Singapore's world-class mathematics system (and what Singapore can learn from the United States): An exploratory study.* American Institutes for Research: Washington, D.C.

Full report available:
http://www.air.org/news/documents/Singapore%20Report%20(Bookmark%20Version).pdf

Huat, J.N. & Huat, L.K. (2001). *A handbook for mathematics teachers in primary schools.* Singapore: Times Media Private Unlimited.

Ma, L. (1999). *Knowing and teaching elementary mathematics: Teachers' understanding of fundamental mathematics in China and the United States.* Mahwah, NJ: Lawrence Erlbaum Assoc., Pub.

National Center for Education Statistics. *Trends in international mathematics and science study 2007.* Full report available: http://nces.ed.gov/timss/

National Council of Teachers of Mathematics. *Standards and Focal Points.* http://www.nctm.org/standards.

National Mathematics Advisory Panel. (2008). *Foundations for success: The final report of the National Mathematics Advisory Panel.* U.S. Department of Education: Washington, DC.

Full report available: http://www.ed.gov/about/bdscomm/list/mathpanel/index.html

Norton, Oak. *Weapons of Math Destruction Comics* http://www.weaponsofmathdestruction.com/index.cfm

Primary Mathematics. U.S. Edition & Standards Edition www.singaporemath.com

Yeap, B. H. (2010). *Bar modeling, a problem-solving tool: From research to practice, an effective math strategy.* Singapore, Marshall Cavendish Education

Yee, L. P. ed. (2007). *Teaching primary school mathematics: A resource book.* Singapore: McGraw Hill.

Yee, L. P. ed. (2007). *Teaching secondary school mathematics: A resource book. (2nd Ed.)* Singapore: McGraw Hill.

Singapore Math Materials:

Earlybird Kindergarten Mathematics Standards Edition consists of:

- Textbook Parts A & B (Includes Math at Home activities)
- Activity Book Parts A & B
- Teacher's Guide Parts A and B & Teacher's Resource Pack
- Posters
- Big Books (Also available as Readers)

Primary Mathematics Standards Edition Grades 1 - 6 consists of:

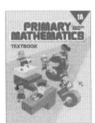

- Textbook Parts A & B
- Workbook Parts A & B
- Extra Practice
- Tests Part A & B
- Teacher's Guide Parts A and B
- Posters (grades 1-3)

This edition is being redone to align to Common Core State Standards, expected publication date is January 2014.

Primary Mathematics U.S Edition Grades 1 - 6 consists of:

- Textbook Parts A & B
- Workbook Parts A & B
- Extra practice
- Teacher's Guide Parts A and B

Math in Focus Grades k - 6 consists of:

- Student Book Parts A & B
- Workbook Parts A & B
- Teacher's Edition Parts A and B
- Extra Practice
- Assessment
- Reteach
- Enrichment

The Singapore Model Method

Written by the Ministry of Education, this book (or monograph, as they refer to the publication) is a comprehensive overview of the Model Method and provides examples for both basic and quite challenging word problems.

"The main purpose is to make explicit how the Model Method is used to develop students' understanding of fundamental mathematics concepts and proficiency in solving basic mathematics word problems." — *Back cover*

Teaching of Whole Numbers: From Research to Practice.

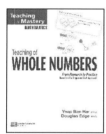

Written for mathematics educators interested in authentic professional learning, this book provides learning opportunities in both content and pedagogy. Backed by research studies and learning theories, the book includes mathematical tasks as well as pedagogical ones to help readers link content and pedagogy.

Teaching of Fractions: From Research to Practice.

Parents and educators will find this an invaluable resource to help develop in students a comprehensive understanding of fractions and how fractions relate to whole numbers, and basic operations involving fractions.

Bar Modeling, a Problem-solving Tool.

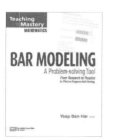

Written for mathematics educators who are interested in learning more about bar modeling as a problem-solving tool in mathematics by leading mathematics education professor at Singapore's National Institute of Education, Yeap Ban Har.

Primary Mathematics Challenging Word Problems for Grades 1 - 6

- Follows the U.S. Edition of primary Mathematics topics.
- Includes topical problems, worked examples, review problems, practice and challenging problems.

Primary Mathematics Intensive Practice for Grades 1 - 6

- Follows the U.S. Edition of primary Mathematics topics
- Part A & B at each level.
- Includes topical, mid-year and end-of-year review, challenging problems.

Process Skills in Problem Solving Grades 1 - 6

- Examples and practice problems for many heuristics as well as in-depth examples of the model method.
- Model Method is used in the 1st & 2nd grade level.

MathExpress: Speed Maths Strategies for Grades 1 - 6

- Demonstrates multiple strategies for working with the four operations.
- Helps students improve mental math speed and accuracy.
- Each strategy has 2 worked examples, practice items and a speed & accuracy assessment.

Singapore Math Practice for Grades 1 - 7

- Introduction explaining Singapore Math method and common problem types.
- Extra practice for students familiar with Singapore Math
- Direct complement to current textbooks used in Singapore
- Part A & B at each level.
- Step-by-step solutions in the answer key.

Singapore Math 70 Must Know Word problems for Grades 2 - 7

- Introduction explaining Singapore Math method.
- One problem per page so as not to overwhelm students.
- Common word problems found on assessments.
- Step-by-step solutions in the answer key.

Step-by-Step Problem Solving for Grades 2 - 7

- Introduction explaining Singapore Math method.
- Focus on the process of problem solving.
- "Think, solve, and answer" format.
- Step-by-step solutions in the answer key
- Each book is 64 pages
-

Singapore Math Mental Math for Grades 2 – 7

- Computation quick tips, thinking shortcuts
- various types of math problems to develop thinking and analytical skills
- Each book is 64 pages

Number Discs

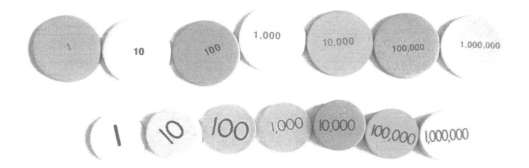

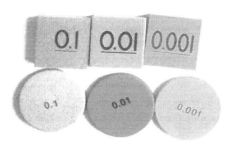

Number disc quality varies depending on manufacturer. You can always make your own with laminated colored paper or fun foam.

Place value cards or strips

Make your own Place Value cards with sentence strips.

KINDERGARTEN:

- ✓ Materials from the classroom including stuffed or plastic animals, kitchen play
- ✓ Various types of counters/buttons/shells/beans
- ✓ Linking cubes
- ✓ Simple balance scale
- ✓ Number cards/ Dot cards/Domino cards
- ✓ Solid shapes or Geometric solids
- ✓ Clock with geared hands
- ✓ Straws/craft sticks/pipe cleaners
- ✓ Picture cards/ cutouts
- ✓ Pipe cleaners/beads
- ✓ Play dough or clay

GRADE 1

- ✓ Individual white board and dry-erase markers
- ✓ Linking cubes
- ✓ Counters or other objects
- ✓ Number cubes or dice or polyhedral dice
- ✓ Base-10 blocks
- ✓ Place-value cards – ones and tens
- ✓ Solid shapes or Geometric Solids (cube, cylinder, cone, rectangular and triangular prism, pyramid, can use toy blocks, objects in classroom)
- ✓ Clock with geared hands
- ✓ Simple balance scale
- ✓ Number cards 0-20, numerals and number words
- ✓ Number cards 0-10, (4 sets) for games (Can use playing cards or uno cards)
- ✓ Index cards – for making number cards and fact cards, or use blank playing cards
- ✓ Fact cards – addition and subtraction through 20
- ✓ Coins and bills
- ✓ Paper plates or bowls for sorting

GRADE 2

- ✓ Individual white board and dry-erase markers
- ✓ Linking cubes
- ✓ Counters
- ✓ Number cubes or dice or polyhedral dice
- ✓ Base-10 blocks

- ✓ Place-value discs (discs labeled 1 – 1000)
- ✓ Place-value chart (draw one on a white-board or paper within a sleeve protector)
- ✓ Place-value cards
- ✓ Measuring tools: Meter and yard stick, Ruler, Measuring tape. Kilogram and gram weights; Pound and ounce weights; Scale in grams and ounces. Liter, quart, pint, and cup liquid containers, other liquid containers
- ✓ Number cards 0-10, 4 sets for games (Can use playing cards or uno cards)
- ✓ Index cards – for making number cards and fact cards, or use blank playing cards
- ✓ Fact cards – addition and subtraction through 20
- ✓ Fact cards – multiplication and division for 2, 3, 4, 5, and 10
- ✓ Drinking straws or toothpicks for regrouping
- ✓ Coins and bills

GRADE 3

- ✓ Individual white board and dry-erase marker
- ✓ Linking cubes
- ✓ Number cubes or dice or polyhedral dice
- ✓ Hundreds chart
- ✓ Base-10 blocks
- ✓ Place-value discs (discs labeled 1 – 10,000)
- ✓ Place-value cards
- ✓ Place-value chart (draw one on a white-board or paper within a sleeve protector)
- ✓ Fraction circles/bars/Pattern Blocks
- ✓ Clock with geared hands
- ✓ Graph paper
- ✓ Measuring tools: Meter and yard stick, Ruler, Measuring tape. Kilogram and gram weights, Pound and ounce weights. Scale in grams and ounces
- ✓ Square tiles (can cut from paper)
- ✓ Centimeter cubes (can use unit cubes from base-10 set)
- ✓ Number cards 0-10, 4 sets for games (Can use playing cards or uno cards)
- ✓ Index cards – for making number cards and fact cards, or use blank playing cards
- ✓ Fact cards – multiplication and division through 10 x 10

GRADE 4

- ✓ Individual white board and dry-erase markers
- ✓ Linking cubes
- ✓ Number cubes or dice or polyhedral dice

- ✓ Place-value discs
- ✓ Place-value chart (draw one on a white-board or paper within a sleeve protector)
- ✓ Decimal number discs (discs labeled with 0.001, 0.01. 0.1)
- ✓ Place-value cards: whole number and decimal
- ✓ Fraction bars
- ✓ Graph paper; Square and isometric dot paper
- ✓ Measuring tools: Meter and yard stick. Ruler
- ✓ Centimeter cubes (can use unit cubes from base-10 set)
- ✓ Protractor
- ✓ Set-square (plastic triangle with one 90 degree angle)
- ✓ 2-color counters (or coins)
- ✓ Number cards 0-10, 4 sets for games (Can use playing cards or uno cards)
- ✓ Index cards — for making number cards and fact cards, or use blank playing cards

GRADE 5

- ✓ Individual white board and dry-erase markers
- ✓ Number cubes or dice or polyhedral dice
- ✓ Place-value discs
- ✓ Place-value chart (draw one on a white-board or paper within a sleeve protector)
- ✓ Decimal number discs (discs labeled with 0.001, 0.01. 0.1)
- ✓ Solid shapes or Geometric Solids
- ✓ Graph paper; X-Y coordinate graphs
- ✓ Ruler
- ✓ Centimeter cubes (can use unit cubes from base-10 set)
- ✓ Protractor
- ✓ Number cards 0-10, 4 sets for games (Can use playing cards or uno cards)
- ✓ Index cards — for making number cards and fact cards, or use blank playing cards.

GRADE 6

- ✓ Individual white board and dry-erase markers
- ✓ Linking cubes
- ✓ Number cubes or dice or polyhedral dice
- ✓ X-Y coordinate graphs
- ✓ Ruler
- ✓ Protractor
- ✓ Set-square (plastic triangle with one 90 degree angle)
- ✓ 2-color counters (or coins)

Singapore Mathematics Websites

Thinking Blocks   http://www.thinkingblocks.com/

> Model your own word problems or work through samples problems. The site also has videos and great number sense games.

The Singapore Maths Teacher   http://www.thesingaporemaths.com

> Sample lessons for grades 3 – 6, published by former Singapore educators.

Math Buddies Online Curriculum   http://www.mconline.us

> Primary Mathematics Online is a web-delivered Singapore math curriculum for grades K-6. Designed to supplement the Singapore Math textbooks, it is correlated to Primary Mathematics Standards Edition and U.S. Edition textbooks, making it easy to integrate into instructional programs.

Interactive Singapore Math   http://www.isingaporemath.com/

> Online tutoring program for students in grade k-5 based on Singapore Math. (Fee based)

Math Buddy Online   http://www.mathbuddyonline.com

> Fee-based program with interactive activities and assessments. Free question of the day based on grade level.

Hey Math!   http://heymath.com

> Fee-based program based in India, HeyMath! is the #1 E-Learning program for Math in 51 countries.

Conceptua Math   http://conceptuamath.com

> Free fraction tools and lessons for use in the classroom. Additional fee-based lessons also. Whole number tools available soon.

Ping! Beep! Ping Beep!

Ping! Beep! Ping Beep! is a good game for working multiplication facts, multiples and common multiples. It is easy to adapt to large and small groups and to make up different versions.

Have the class or a group stand. Begin by having students count off, starting with one. When introducing the game, you might want to do each step separately. When students are familiar, just give them a pair of numbers and skip straight to Ping! Beep! The basic rules are:

1. Students say "Ping!" as a substitute for a multiple of a selected number. For example, if the Ping! number is 3, students will count off:

   1, 2, Ping!, 4, 5, Ping!, etc.

2. Students say "Beep!" as a substitute for a multiple of a second selected number. For example, if the Beep! number is 4, students will count off:

   1, 2, 3, Beep!, 5, 6, 7, Beep!, 9, etc.

3. Add in the common multiples of the chosen numbers substituting "Ping Beep!". Using the numbers 3 and 4 from the prior steps, our sequence would be:

   1, 2, Ping!, Beep!, 5, Ping!, 7, Beep!, Ping!, 10, 11, Ping Beep!, 13, etc.

4. One way to end the game: if a student loses track of where the class is in counting, that student sits down. Last one standing wins.

With younger students, simply use Ping! for multiples. The fun really starts when counting passes the multiples of 10!

Magic Math Hand

Or Magic Thumb or make up your own name! Simply ask students to count in different ways **both** up and down the number line by aiming your thumb up or down. No need to start at zero. For example:

Count by 4's beginning at 3 might look like:

   3, 7, 11, 15, 11, 15, 19, 23, 27, 31, 35, 31, 27, 23, 19, 23

Count by tenths beginning at .8:

   8 tenths, 9 tenths, 1, 1 and 1 tenth, 1, 9 tenths, 1, 1 and 1 tenth, 1 and 2 tenths...

Buddy Hands/Show me the Bond

Using the concept of a Number Bond, have students show you their "part of a bond when given the whole (10) and one part. For example: Tell students "We're going to make number bonds to 10. My part is 4; show me on your hands what your part is."

For numbers greater than 10, have the students use individual whiteboards to show you their part. You can use a simple number bond on the class whiteboard.
Examples:

Let's make bonds to 20.
My part is 5, show me your part.

Let's make bonds to 100.
My part is 35, show me your part.

Let's make bonds to 200.
My part is 135, show me your part.

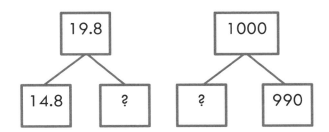

Hundreds Chart Game

This game can be played by two – four players. One player will shuffle a set of number cards with digits 0-9 and place them face down in the center.

Each player selects 4 cards and arranges them into 2, two digit numbers with a sum less than 100. Zero can be used in the tens place.

Choose a player to begin. When the student has added his two numbers together, the answer is covered up on the hundreds chart.

If a number has already been covered, the player must rearrange his or her digits to make a new sum. If this cannot be done, the player may exchange 1 card for one off the top of the pile.

The game continues until a player gets three counters in a row. Students can cooperate in determining how to arrange the cards so that the sum is not a number that is already covered up.

Salute!

Materials needed: Deck of cards

Number of players: 3

Salute is played with 3 students and a deck of cards. For younger students, remove the face cards. Split the deck in half and give each pile to two of the players. The third player is the Caller. When the Caller says "Salute!" the players place the top card from their pile on their forehead to salute each other. Each of the two players can see the others card, but not their own. The Caller tells them the SUM of the two numbers on the players' cards. (Think of the three as a number bond with one of the addends missing.)

The aim of the game is for the players to tell the number shown on their own cards, which they cannot see. First correct answer wins. Winners can collect the two cards or players can play through their pile or take turns being the Caller.

The game can be modified for subtraction or multiplication. The pictures on the playing cards can help students that aren't solid on their facts by counting the items. To make the game more challenging, create a set of blank cards.

Make 10

Remove the tens, jacks, queens and kings from a standard deck of cards.
Deal 9 cards face up in a square grid.

A player may capture by calling out "ten" and taking any pair of cards that add up to 10. When no more captures are available, replace spaces with cards from the deck. Game continues until all cards are used. Winner is the person with the most captures. *(Tip: Uno number cards also work well!)*

Variations:
1. Change capture to two or three cards that add up to 15.
2. Change capture to three or more cards that add up to 21.
3. Play with 10s, Jacks (11), Queens (12) and Kings (13) with a target of 15.
4. Set your own target total

Number Strings

Number strings are short mental math activities designed so that students work several calculations in their head then provide the answer in chorus, either verbally, with whiteboards, fingers or pencil and paper. Have students write their answer on an individual whiteboard and place it upside down on their desks. (To avoid excessive drawing, remind students that you want to hear their marker "click"!)

When directed, students will show their answer to the teacher, who immediately checks for comprehension and enthusiastically provides an answer to each student ("I challenge your answer" or "Yes!").

In addition to providing a teacher with instant formative assessment, number strings offer the opportunity to integrate mathematics throughout the curriculum. Use the following samples or write your own!

Sample number strings

Start with the number of halves in a whole.	2
Double it. (2 + 2)	4
Add the number of sides on a triangle. (4 + 3)	7
Subtract the number of legs on a healthy horse. (7 - 4)	3
Triple that number. (3 x 3)	9
Multiple by the number of sides on a rectangle. (9 x 4)	36
Subtract the number of days in a week. (36 − 7)	**29**

Begin with the number of hours in a day.	24
Subtract 4. (24 - 4)	20
Divide by 2. (20 ÷ 2)	10
Add the number of legs on an octopus. (10 + 8)	18
Subtract a dozen. (18 − 12)	6
Divide by 3. (6 ÷ 3)	2
Divide by the number of thumbs on your hands. (2 ÷ 2)	**1**

Sample number strings tied to curriculum

Start with the number of letters in the name of the continent on which we live. (OK to write "North America" on the board.)	12
Add the number of letters in the name of the ocean bordering the east coast of the United States. (12 + 8) (Atlantic)	20
Divide by 2 (20 ÷ 2)	**10**

Take the number of sides on a rectangle.	4
Add the number of sides on a square (4 + 4)	8
Add that number to the number of sides on a triangle. (8 + 3)	**11**

Begin with the number of incisors on the top of your mouth.	4
Add the number of incisors on the bottom of your mouth. (4 + 4)	8
Add the total number of canine teeth (8 + 4)	**12**

Begin with the number of continents on Earth.	7
Multiply by the number of oceans on Earth (7 x 5)	35
Subtract the number of Cardinal Directions on a Compass Rose	**31**

Begin with the number of consuls that ruled Rome at one time.	2
Multiply by the number of brothers that founded Rome	4
Add the number of hills that surround Rome (4 + 7= 11)?	11
Multiply by the Roman Numeral V (11 x 5)	**55**

Begin with the number of legs on an ant.	6
Multiply by the number of legs on a spider (6 x 8)	48
Divide by the number of legs on a human (48 ÷ 2)	24
Divide by the number of legs on a healthy iguana (24 ÷ 4)	**6**

Take the number of hemispheres in your brain.	2
Multiply by the number of bones in your ear. (2 x 3)	6
Multiply by the number of your senses. (6 x 5)	30
Multiply that number by 6. (6 x 30)	**180**

Begin with the number of days in a leap year.	366
Subtract the number of months in a year. (366 − 12)	354
Subtract the number of days in January. (354 - 31)	323
Add the number of days in a week. (323 + 7)	**330**

These card sets can be created for many topics and can be used as a whole class or a center activity for partners or small groups. Hand out the 20 cards to children. If there are less than 20 children, give more cards to the children. The first child reads one of their cards i.e., 'I have 15, who has   7 + 3, the child who has 10 then continues until the circle is complete. It is a fun game that keeps everyone engaged trying to figure out the answers.

It's always a good idea to have a key!

Mathwire.com has many premade sets of these decks available for teachers in a pdf file including:

- Multiplication Facts
- Multiplication Facts (Spanish version)
- Multiplication Facts, Deck B [harder facts: 5 through 12 times tables]
- Who Has? Multiplication Deck C practices the 2, 5 and 10 times tables.
- Who Has? Multiplication Deck D practices the 0, 1 and 2 times tables.
- Addition Deck (25 cards)
- Who Has? Doubles deck formatted to print on 2x4 inch labels which can easily be affixed to index cards to create the deck.
- Who Has? Doubles deck
- More or Less Deck
- Fractions Deck
- Base Ten Deck
- Place Value Deck
- Coins
- Algebra Variable Expression Deck

KEY

1. I have 1. Who has 17 times as many?
1. I have 17. Who has this less 1?
2. I have 16. Who has double this?
3. I have 32. Who has this take away 5?
4. I have 27. Who has this divided by 9, multiplied by 10?
5. I have 30. Who has this times 2?
6. I have 60. Who has this divided by 12 less 3?
7. I have 2. Who has this and 2 more?
8. I have 4. Who has twice as many?
9. I have 8. Who has 3 times as many?
10. I have 24. Who has 1/4 of this?
11. I have 6. Who has this plus 3?
12. I have 9. Who has this divided by 3?
13. I have 3. Who has a dozen more?
14. I have 15. Who has this multiplied by 2 minus 11?
15. I have 19. Who has this minus 2 plus a dozen more?
16. I have 29. Who has this plus 33 divided by 2?
17. I have 31. Who has this less 5?
18. I have 26. Who has this divided by 2 plus 20?
19. I have 33. Who has this divided by 3 and 11 more?
20. I have 22. Who has this less 2?
21. I have 20. Who has ¼ of this?
22. I have 5. Who has 5 more?
23. I have 10. Who has 3 less?
24. I have 7. Who has this and 7 more?
25. I have 14. Who has double this?
26. I have 28. Who has 5 less?
27. I have 23. Who has this less 1 and divided by 2?
28. I have 11. Who has 1 more?
29.   I have 12. Who has ½ as many more?
30. I have 18. Who has 5 less?
31. I have 13. Who has a dozen more?
32. I have 25. Who has 4 less?
33. I have 21. Who has 20 less?

I have 1. Who has 17 times as many?

I have 17. Who has this less 1?

I have 16. Who has double this?

I have 32. Who has this take away 5?

I have 27. Who has this divided by 9, multiplied by 10?

I have 30. Who has this times 2?

I have 60. Who has this divided by 12 less 3?

I have 2. Who has this and 2 more?

I have 4. Who has twice as many?

I have 8. Who has 3 times as many?

I have 24. Who has 1/4 of this?

I have 6. Who has this plus 3?

I have 9. Who has this divided by 3?

I have 3. Who has a dozen more?

I have 15. Who has this multiplied by 2 minus 11?

I have 19. Who has this minus 2 plus a dozen more?

I have 29. Who has this plus 33 divided by 2?

I have 31.

Who has this less 5?

I have 26. Who has this divided by 2 plus 20?

I have 33. Who has this divided by 3 and 11 more?

I have 22.

Who has this less 2?

I have 20.

Who has ¼ of this?

I have 5.

Who has 5 more?

I have 10.

Who has 3 less?

I have 7. Who has this and 7 more?

I have 14. Who has double this?

I have 28. Who has 5 less?

I have 23. Who has this less 1 and divided by 2?

I have 11. Who has 1 more?

I have 12. Who has ½ as many more?

I have 18. Who has 5 less?

I have 13. Who has a dozen more?

I have 25. Who has 4 less?

I have 21. Who has 20 less?

Other versions available online at adrianbruce.com (x7, x8, x9)

6	24	48	18
42	12	60	54
36	0	0	30

1. Copy and cut out the multiplication cards on the following pages.

2. Draw the above grid on concrete using chalk. Each square should be about 30cm by 30cm.

3. Two players stand with their feet in the large feet facing the game board.

4. A 'Caller' asks a question from one of the cards.

5. When a player has worked out the answer they must jump from their spot onto the correct answer. Do not move until you know the answer.

6. Players then rotate positions but the winner stays to compete with next player.

6 x 0 =	0 x 6 =
6 x 1 =	1 x 6 =
2 x 6 =	6 x 2 =
6 x 3 =	3 x 6 =
6 x 4 =	4 x 6 =
6 x 5 =	5 x 6 =

6 x 6 =	6 x 7 =
7 x 6 =	6 x 8 =
8 x 6 =	6 x 9 =
9 x 6 =	6 x 10 =
10 x 6 =	

 # How to give a sprint

1. Hand out, face-down, a SPRINT to complete in 1 minute. Instruct students not to turn the sheet face-up until told to "GO!" Get students excited and start them enthusiastically: "On your mark, get set, GO!" Begin timer.

2. When timer rings indicating one minute has elapsed, instruct students to:

    a) Stop working
    b) Draw a line under the last problem they have completed
    c) Put pencils down

3. Read off the correct answers while students pump their hand in the air and respond "**yes**" to each problem that was answered correctly. They should be silent for any incorrect answers. (Shouting "NO" is bad karma!)

4. Tell students to mark the number of correct problems at the top of the page. Ask how many students got at least one right on their "sprint." (All hands should raise.) Two right? Three? Continue until there is only one hand left in the air and applaud for that person.

5. Tell students to take a couple of minutes to refocus on the math and complete the worksheet.

6. Tell students to stand-up, push in their chairs and make sure they have some space.

7. Then lead them in chorally skip counting (10, 20, 30, etc.) while completing an exercise known as cross crawl. In this exercise, students raise their left knee to their right elbow, then the right knee to the left elbow. Other exercises can be utilized that cross the midline, such as windmills, Macarena, etc.

8. Hurry students back to their seats and hand them another worksheet, face-down.

9. Repeat the preceding procedure through step four.

10. Now have students compare their two scores and ask, "How many of you completed **at least** one question more on the second sprint?" Hands should all raise. "Two better? Keep your hands up...Three better?... four?" and so on until only one person has their hand in the air. Applaud for the person who was the "most improved."

11. Instruct participants to toss both halves of the sprint in the trash. It is important to let students know that this is simply a competition against oneself to improve basic math facts and it is for fun. It is NOT for a grade.

A good sprint:

1. Consists of two halves which test the same ONE skill.
2. Builds in difficulty.
3. Is challenging enough that no one will be able to finish it in a minute.

BY THE WAY: Students in Singapore have probably never heard of this type of sprint. This is an American activity designed to assist our students in mental math skills. Singaporean parents are diligent in preparing their children for success in mathematics and feel that it is their responsibility to aid the teachers with this skill. Generally speaking, parents in our country expect that math facts will be mastered in the classroom.

Sample Sprint 1

1.	28 + 2 =	16.	74 – 39 =
2.	28 + 12 =	17.	55 + 28 =
3.	28 + 22 =	18.	73 + 19 =
4.	28 + 42 =	19.	13 + 49 =
5.	17 + 33 =	20.	7 + 86 =
6.	57 – 22 =	21.	57 + 23 =
7.	97 - 45 =	22.	99 + 62 =
8.	46 - 25 =	23.	47 + 39 =
9.	42 + 54 =	24.	59 + 37 =
10.	37 + 31 =	25.	83 - 39 =
11.	37 + 24 =	26.	29 + 71 =
12.	66 + 8 =	27.	97 + 44 =
13.	66 + 18 =	28.	79 + 98 =
14.	66 + 19 =	29.	87 + 87 =
15.	82 – 48 =	30.	821 - 76 =

1.	$38 + 2 =$		16.	$84 - 39 =$
2.	$38 + 12 =$		17.	$45 + 38 =$
3.	$38 + 22 =$		18.	$63 + 29 =$
4.	$38 + 42 =$		19.	$23 + 49 =$
5.	$27 + 33 =$		20.	$7 + 76 =$
6.	$67 - 22 =$		21.	$47 + 23 =$
7.	$98 - 45 =$		22.	$99 + 72 =$
8.	$56 - 25 =$		23.	$47 + 49 =$
9.	$32 + 64 =$		24.	$59 + 27 =$
10.	$47 + 41 =$		25.	$83 - 29 =$
11.	$37 + 34 =$		26.	$29 + 61 =$
12.	$76 + 8 =$		27.	$97 + 34 =$
13.	$76 + 18 =$		28.	$79 + 98 =$
14.	$76 + 19 =$		29.	$77 + 77 =$
15.	$72 - 48 =$		30.	$821 - 57 =$

What number is missing?   (1)

1. 1, _____, 3

2. 2, 3, _____

3. 5, 6, _____, 8

4. 7, 8, _____

5. 3, 4, _____, 6

6. 2, _____, 4

7. 4, _____, 6

8. 6, 7, _____

9. 7, _____, 9

10. _____, 3, 4, 5

11. 1, 2, _____

12. 3, _____, 5, 6

13. 4, 5, _____

14. 5, 6, 7, _____

15. 6, _____, 8

16. 3, 2, _____

17. 4, 3, _____, 1

18. 7, _____, 5

19. 9, 8, _____

20. 10, _____, 8, 7

21. 5, 4, _____

22. 6, _____, 4

23. 7, 6, _____

24. 10, 9, _____

25. 9, _____, 7

26. _____, 6, 5, 4

27. _____, 4, 3, 2

28. _____, 9, 8

29. _____, 6, 5

30. 3, 2, 1, _____

What number is missing?   (2)

1. 1, 2, _____,

2. 3, _____, 5

3. 5, 6, 7, _____,

4. _____, 8, 9

5. 4, 5, _____

6. _____, 4, 5

7. _____, 6, 7

8. 7, _____, 9

9. 8, 9, _____

10. _____, 4, 5

11. 1, 2, _____

12. 3, _____, 5, 6

13. 5, _____, 7

14. 5, 6, 7, _____

15. 6, _____, 8

16. 4, 3, 2, _____

17. 4, _____, 2

18. _____, 5, 4

19. 9, 8, _____

20. 10, 9, _____, 7

21. 5, 4, _____

22. 6, 5, _____

23. 7, 6, _____

24. 10, 9, _____

25. 10, 9, _____

26. 8, 7, _____

27. _____, 4, 3, 2

28. _____, 9, 8

29. 6, 5, _____

30. 3, 2, 1, _____

Multiply. (1)

1.	4 x 1 =	16.	9 x 4 =
2.	4 x 2 =	17.	4 x 10 =
3.	4 x 3 =	18.	4 x 0 =
4.	1 x 4 =	19.	4 x 9 =
5.	2 x 4 =	20.	8 x 4 =
6.	3 x 4 =	21.	7 x 4 =
7.	5 x 4 =	22.	4 x 6 =
8.	6 x 4 =	23.	10 x 4 =
9.	4 x 7 =	24.	4 x 9 =
10.	4 x 8 =	25.	4 x 4 =
11.	0 x 4 =	26.	4 x 7 =
12.	2 x 4 =	27.	4 x 10 =
13.	4 x 4 =	28.	4 x 11 =
14.	6 x 4 =	29.	4 x 12
15.	8 x 4 =	30.	4 x 13 =

Multiply. (2)

1.	1 x 4 =	16.	9 x 4 =
2.	2 x 4 =	17.	10 x 4 =
3.	4 x 3 =	18.	4 x 0 =
4.	4 x 1 =	19.	4 x 8
5.	4 x 2 =	20.	8 x 4 =
6.	3 x 4 =	21.	7 x 4 =
7.	6 x 4 =	22.	4 x 7 =
8.	4 x 5 =	23.	10 x 4 =
9.	4 x 6 =	24.	4 x 9 =
10.	4 x 7 =	25.	4 x 3 =
11.	0 x 4 =	26.	4 x 2 =
12.	1 x 4 =	27.	10 x 4 =
13.	3 x 4 =	28.	11 x 4 =
14.	5 x 4 =	29.	12 x 4 =
15.	7 x 4 =	30.	13 x 4 =

Add. All answers must be in simplest form.

1.	$\dfrac{1}{3} + \dfrac{1}{3} =$	11.	$\dfrac{2}{5} + \dfrac{1}{10} =$
2.	$\dfrac{1}{5} + \dfrac{1}{5} =$	12.	$\dfrac{3}{8} + \dfrac{1}{4} =$
3.	$\dfrac{1}{6} + \dfrac{1}{6} =$	13.	$\dfrac{3}{8} + \dfrac{1}{2} =$
4.	$\dfrac{1}{4} + \dfrac{1}{2} =$	14.	$\dfrac{5}{6} + \dfrac{1}{6} =$
5.	$\dfrac{1}{2} + \dfrac{1}{2} =$	15.	$\dfrac{1}{7} + \dfrac{3}{7} =$
6.	$\dfrac{1}{4} + \dfrac{1}{4} =$	16.	$\dfrac{1}{7} + \dfrac{5}{14} =$
7.	$\dfrac{1}{8} + \dfrac{3}{8} =$	17.	$\dfrac{1}{8} + \dfrac{1}{16} =$
8.	$\dfrac{1}{10} + \dfrac{1}{10} =$	18.	$\dfrac{2}{3} + \dfrac{1}{9} =$
9.	$\dfrac{1}{10} + \dfrac{1}{5} =$	19.	$\dfrac{5}{12} + \dfrac{5}{12} =$
10.	$\dfrac{1}{10} + \dfrac{7}{10} =$	20.	$\dfrac{1}{3} + \dfrac{2}{3} =$

Add. All answers must be in simplest form. 2

1.	$\frac{1}{5} + \frac{1}{5} =$		11.	$\frac{2}{5} + \frac{3}{10} =$
2.	$\frac{1}{7} + \frac{1}{7} =$		12.	$\frac{1}{8} + \frac{1}{4} =$
3.	$\frac{1}{3} + \frac{1}{3} =$		13.	$\frac{1}{8} + \frac{1}{2} =$
4.	$\frac{1}{4} + \frac{1}{4} =$		14.	$\frac{5}{7} + \frac{2}{7} =$
5.	$\frac{1}{2} + \frac{1}{2} =$		15.	$\frac{1}{7} + \frac{2}{7} =$
6.	$\frac{1}{8} + \frac{1}{8} =$		16.	$\frac{1}{7} + \frac{3}{14} =$
7.	$\frac{1}{8} + \frac{5}{8} =$		17.	$\frac{3}{8} + \frac{1}{16} =$
8.	$\frac{2}{10} + \frac{2}{10} =$		18.	$\frac{1}{3} + \frac{1}{9} =$
9.	$\frac{1}{10} + \frac{2}{5} =$		19.	$\frac{4}{12} + \frac{4}{12} =$
10.	$\frac{1}{10} + \frac{5}{10} =$		20.	$\frac{1}{5} + \frac{4}{5} =$

Answer the following questions. 1

1.	What is $\frac{1}{2}$ of 10?	11.	What is $\frac{1}{5}$ of 10?
2.	What is $\frac{1}{2}$ of 8?	12.	What is $\frac{1}{5}$ of 15?
3.	What is $\frac{1}{2}$ of 12?	13.	What is $\frac{1}{5}$ of 20?
4.	What is $\frac{1}{2}$ of 20?	14.	What is $\frac{1}{5}$ of 30?
5.	What is $\frac{1}{3}$ of 9?	15.	What is $\frac{1}{10}$ of 20?
6.	What is $\frac{1}{3}$ of 12?	16.	What is $\frac{1}{10}$ of 40?
7.	What is $\frac{1}{3}$ of 6?	17.	What is $\frac{1}{3}$ of 9?
8.	What is $\frac{1}{3}$ of 15?	18.	What is $\frac{2}{3}$ of 9?
9.	What is $\frac{1}{4}$ of 8?	19.	What is $\frac{1}{4}$ of 12?
10.	What is $\frac{1}{4}$ of 16?	20.	What is $\frac{3}{4}$ of 12?

Answer the following questions.

1.	What is $\frac{1}{2}$ of 8?	11.	What is $\frac{1}{5}$ of 10?
2.	What is $\frac{1}{2}$ of 6?	12.	What is $\frac{1}{5}$ of 15?
3.	What is $\frac{1}{2}$ of 14?	13.	What is $\frac{1}{5}$ of 20?
4.	What is $\frac{1}{2}$ of 10?	14.	What is $\frac{1}{5}$ of 25?
5.	What is $\frac{1}{3}$ of 9?	15.	What is $\frac{1}{10}$ of 20?
6.	What is $\frac{1}{3}$ of 15?	16.	What is $\frac{1}{10}$ of 30?
7.	What is $\frac{1}{3}$ of 12?	17.	What is $\frac{1}{3}$ of 6?
8.	What is $\frac{1}{3}$ of 18?	18.	What is $\frac{2}{3}$ of 6?
9.	What is $\frac{1}{4}$ of 8?	19.	What is $\frac{1}{4}$ of 8?
10.	What is $\frac{1}{4}$ of 12?	20.	What is $\frac{3}{4}$ of 8?

5 Minute Frenzy

1. Choose operation – additon or multipication.

2. Preprint the first column and top row numbers or have students fill these in on a blank chart. Use popsicle sticks with numbers on them, playing cards, etc. to get random numbers.

3. Have the students complete as many facts as they can in 5 minutes.

4. Charts the number of correct resposnses or have students chart their own.

5. When the entire class or group can complete all of the facts in under 5 minutes, have a 5 minute frenzy party. (This could take months to get to)

6. Shorten to 4.5 minute frenzy and repeat!

Example:

X	6	2	1	0	9	8	5	4	7	3
5										
7										
3										
9										
6										
8										
4										
2										
1										
10										

Five Minute Frenzy

Name:_____
Date: _____

Answers

No Peeking!

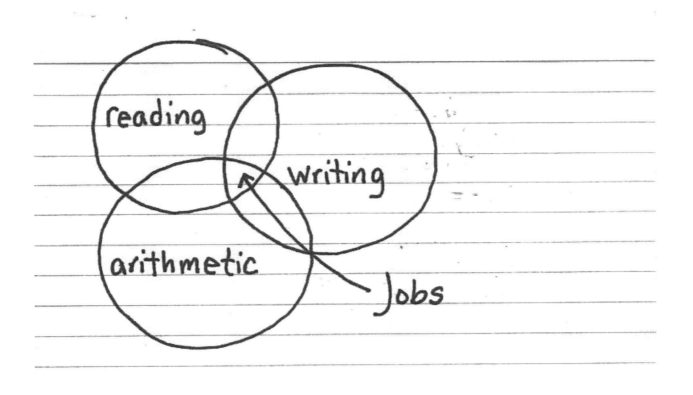

Mental Math Strategies Modeled

Addition

➤ Add two 1-digit numbers whose sum is greater than 10 by making a 10. (This strategy is useful for students who know the addition and subtraction facts through 10, but have trouble memorizing the addition and subtraction facts through 20.)

$7 + 5 = 12$

$7 + 5 = 10 + 2 = 12$ OR $7 + 5 = 10 + 2 = 12$

$3 \quad 2$ $2 \quad 5$

➤ Add tens to 2-digit numbers by adding the tens.

$48 + 20 = 68$

$48 + 20 = 60 + 8 = 68$

$8 \quad 40$

➤ Add a 1-digit number to a 2-digit number; adding the ones results in a number greater than 10 by making a 10 or by using basic addition facts.

$68 + 5 = 73$

$68 + 5 = 70 + 3$ $68 + 5 = 60 + 13 + = 73$

$2 \quad 3$ $60 \quad 8$

➤ Add a 2-digit number to a 2-digit number by making a ten.

$48 + 25 = 73$

$48 + 25 = 50 + 23 = 73$

$2 \quad 23$

128

➢ Add a 2-digit number to a 2-digit number by adding the next ten and then subtract appropriate number of ones.

$$48 + 25 = 73 \qquad\qquad (25+50) - 2 = 75 - 2 = 73$$

➢ Add a number close to 100 by making 100.

$$57 + 98 = 155$$

$$57 + 98 = 55 + 100 = 155$$
$$/\ \quad$$
$$55 \quad 2$$

➢ Add a number close to 100 by first adding 100 and then subtracting the difference.

$$+100 \quad -2$$
$$\searrow \quad \swarrow$$
$$57 + 98 = 155 \qquad\qquad (57 + 100) - 2 = 157 - 2 = 155$$

$$+100 \quad -20$$
$$\searrow \quad \swarrow$$
$$54 + 80 = 154 - 20$$
$$= 134$$

Subtraction

➢ Subtract tens from 2-digit numbers by subtracting the tens.

$$48 - 20 = 28$$

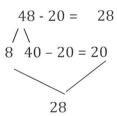

$$48 - 20 = \quad 28$$
$$/\ \quad$$
$$8 \quad 40 - 20 = 20$$
$$28$$

➢ Subtract a 1-digit number from a 2-digit number when there are not enough ones by:

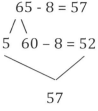

$$65 - 8 = 57$$
$$/ \ $$
$$5 \quad 60 - 8 = 52$$
$$57$$

$$65 - 8 = 57$$
$$/ \ $$
$$50 \quad 15 - 8 = 7$$
$$57$$

- ○ subtracting from 10
- ○ using basic subtraction facts

65 – 8 = 57

➢ Subtract a 2 digit number from a 2 digit number by subtracting from the nearest ten.

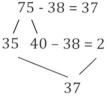

$$75 - 38 = 37$$
$$/ \ $$
$$35 \quad 40 - 38 = 2$$
$$37$$

75 – 38 = 37

➢ Subtract a 2 digit number from a 2 digit number by subtracting the next ten and then adding back in the appropriate number of ones.

$$-40 \quad +2$$

75 – 38 = 37

$$(75 - 40) + 2 = 35 + 2 = 37$$

➢ Subtract a number close to 100 by subtracting 100 and then adding back the difference.

$$-100 \quad +2$$

457 – 98 = 359

$$(457 - 100) + 2 = 359$$

➢ Subtract a number without regrouping

$$999 \quad +1$$

1000 – 364 = 636

$$(999 - 364) + 1 = 635 + 1$$

➢ Subtract using compensation

47 – 19 = 28   47 – 19 = 48 – 20 = 28

Multiplication

➢ Multiply a 2 digit number by a 1-digit number by expanded notation.

10   +3

13 x 4 = 52 $(10 \times 4) + (3 \times 4) = 40 + 12$
$= 52$

➢ Multiply a 2 digit number by a 1-digit number.

79 twos = 80 twos – 1 two

80   -1

79 x 2 = 158 $(80 \times 2) - (1 \times 2) = 160 - 2$
$= 158$

➢ Multiply a 3 digit number by a 1-digit number.

198 threes = 200 threes – 2 threes

200   -2

198 x 3 = 594 $(200 \times 3) - (2 \times 3) = 600 - 6$
$= 594$

➢ Multiplying by 5. 2 fives = 10. Multiply by 10, then half the product.

26 x 5 = 130 $26 \times 10 \div 2 = 260 \div 2$
$= 130$

Division

➤ Divide a number by 2.

Half of 38 = half of 40 − half of 2.

40   -2

$38 \div 2 = 19$ $(40 \div 2) - (2 \div 2) = 20 - 1$

$= 19$

Half of 116 = half of 120 − half of 4.

120   -4

$116 \div 2 = 58$ $(120 \div 2) - (4 \div 2) = 60 - 2$

$= 58$

➤ Divide a number by 5.

$90 \div 5$ = double 90 ÷ double 5.

$90 \div 5 = 18$ $(90 \times 2) \div (5 \times 2) = 180 \div 10$

$= 18$

$320 \div 5$ = double 320 ÷ double 5.

$320 \div 5 = 64$ $(320 \times 2) \div (5 \times 2) = 640 \div 10$

$= 64$

Word Problem Answers

1. The total length of 2 pieces of rope is 18 yds. One piece of rope is 3 yds. long. What is the length of the other piece of rope?

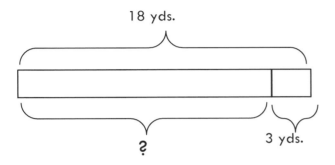

$$18 \text{ yds.} - 3 \text{ yds} = 15 \text{ yds.}$$

The length of the other piece of rope is **15 yds.**

- -

2. Linda has 18 dolls.
   (a) If she puts them on 2 shelves equally, how many dolls does she put on each shelf?

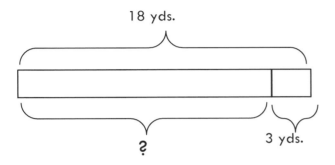

$$18 \div 2 = 9$$

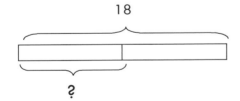

She puts **9** dolls on each shelf.

   (b) If she puts them on 3 shelves equally, how many dolls does she put on each shelf?

$$18 \div 3 = 6$$

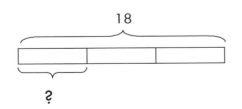

She puts **6** dolls on each shelf.

133

3. *4 children bought a present for $28. They shared the cost equally. How much did each child pay?*

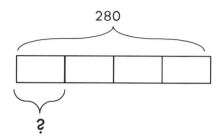

$28 ÷ 4 = $7

Each child paid **$7.**

4. *Kendra made 280 egg salad sandwiches for a party. She made 3 times as many chicken sandwiches as egg salad sandwiches. How many chicken sandwiches did she make?*

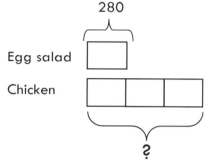

Egg salad

Chicken

280 x 3 = 840

Kendra made **840** chicken sandwiches.

5. *A fruit seller had 1136 oranges. 16 of them were rotten. He packed the rest into 8 boxes. How many oranges were in each box?*

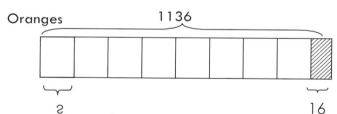

Step 1: How many oranges?

Step 2: How many boxes?

1136 − 16 = 1120 There were 1120 oranges.

1120 ÷ 8 = 140 **There were 140 oranges in each box.**

6. Aaron and Ben have 825 Pokémon cards altogether. If Aaron has 79 Pokémon cards less than Ben, how many Pokémon cards does Ben have?

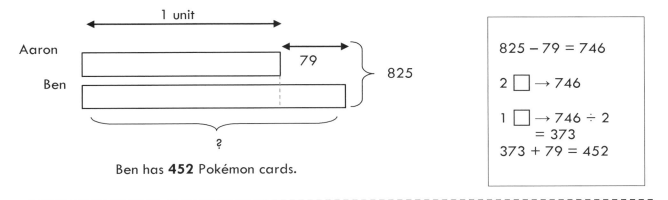

Ben has **452** Pokémon cards.

$$825 - 79 = 746$$

$$2 \,\square \rightarrow 746$$

$$1 \,\square \rightarrow 746 \div 2$$
$$= 373$$
$$373 + 79 = 452$$

---

7. Matt bought 5 times as many apples as Cecelia. Wilson bought 125 apples more than Cecilia. The three children had 1000 apples in all. How many apples did Wilson buy?

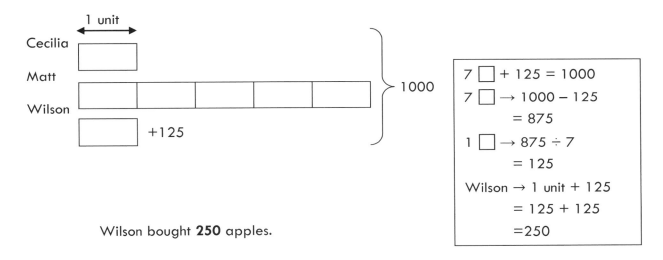

Wilson bought **250** apples.

$$7 \,\square + 125 = 1000$$

$$7 \,\square \rightarrow 1000 - 125$$
$$= 875$$

$$1 \,\square \rightarrow 875 \div 7$$
$$= 125$$

Wilson → 1 unit + 125
$$= 125 + 125$$
$$= 250$$

---

8. The difference between two numbers is 2,184. If the bigger number is 3 times the smaller number, find the sum of the two numbers.

First number

Second number

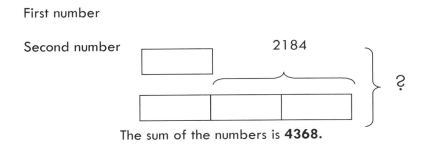

The sum of the numbers is **4368**.

$$2184 \times 2 = 4368$$

or

$$2 \,\square \rightarrow 2184$$

$$1 \,\square \rightarrow 2184 \div 2 = 1092$$

$$4 \,\square \rightarrow 1092 \times 4 = 4368$$

9. *After Jolene had given 128 stickers to Lynn, they had the same number of stickers. If they had 448 stickers altogether, how many stickers did Jolene have at first?*

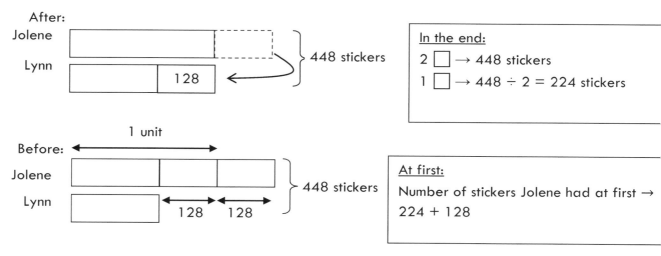

After:
Jolene
Lynn

448 stickers

In the end:
2 ☐ → 448 stickers
1 ☐ → 448 ÷ 2 = 224 stickers

1 unit

Before:
Jolene
Lynn

448 stickers

At first:
Number of stickers Jolene had at first →
224 + 128

Jolene had **352** stickers at first.

---

10. There were 48 chocolates in a box. After eating some of them, Tara found that she had $\frac{5}{8}$ of the chocolates left. How many chocolates did she eat?

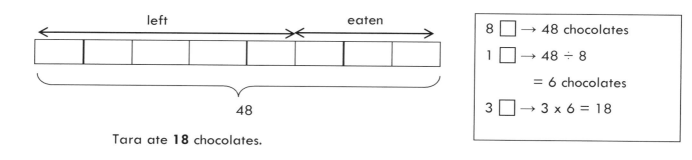

left   eaten

48

8 ☐ → 48 chocolates
1 ☐ → 48 ÷ 8
      = 6 chocolates
3 ☐ → 3 x 6 = 18

Tara ate **18** chocolates.

---

11. *Steve bought 2 bottles of orange juice and a bottle of apple juice for $6.55. The bottle of apple juice cost $0.35 less than the bottle of orange juice. What was the cost of one bottle of orange juice?*

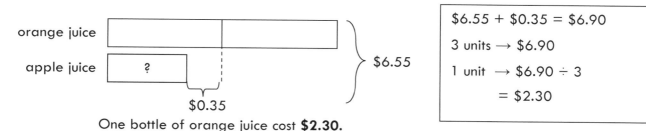

orange juice
apple juice
?
$0.35

$6.55

$6.55 + $0.35 = $6.90
3 units → $6.90
1 unit → $6.90 ÷ 3
       = $2.30

One bottle of orange juice cost **$2.30.**

12. Tyrone bought a bag of marbles. $\frac{1}{4}$ of the marbles were blue, $\frac{1}{8}$ were green, and $\frac{1}{5}$ of the remainder were yellow. If there were 24 yellow marbles, how many marbles did he buy?

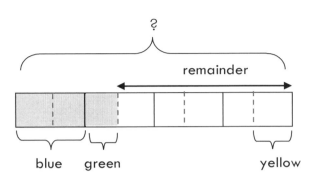

Tyrone bought **192** marbles.

Divide total marbles into quarters.

Divide each quarter in half to find eighths.

$\frac{1}{5}$ of the remainder → 1 unit

24 marbles → 1 unit

24 x 8 units = 192

- -

13. William had $500. He spent 24% of his money on transport and 36% on food.
    (a) What percentage of his money was left?

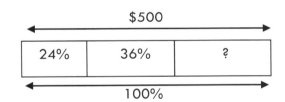

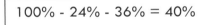

100% - 24% - 36% = 40%

William had **40%** of his money left.

(b) How much money was left?

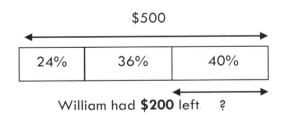

40 % x $500 = $200

William had **$200** left. ?

137

14. Ian has $56. Brandon has 20% more money than Ian. How much money does Brandon have?

0%   100%   120%

Ian $56

Brandon

?

Brandon has **$67.20.**

Brandon's money is 120% of Ian's money.

$$120\% \text{ of } \$56 = \frac{120}{100} \times \$56$$

$$= \$?$$

- -

15. The ratio of the number of Jimmy's marbles to the number of Kelvin's marbles was 3:4. After Jimmy bought another 60 marbles, he had twice as many marbles as Kelvin. How many marbles did Jimmy have at first?

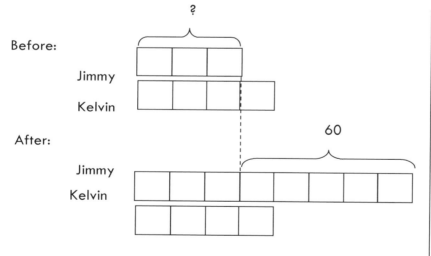

Before:
    Jimmy
    Kelvin

After:
    Jimmy
    Kelvin

Jimmy's 60 more marbles change the ratio from 3:4 to 2:1 (or 8:4)

5 ☐ → 60 marbles

1 ☐ → 60 ÷ 5 = 12 marbles

3 ☐ → 3 x 12 = 36 marbles

Jimmy had **36 marbles** at first.

138

16. The average weight of Henry, Peter and John is 35.5 kg. Peter is twice as heavy as John. Henry is 4kg lighter than Peter. Find Peter's weight.

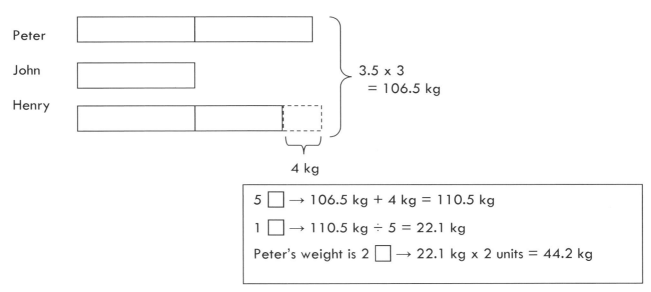

$5 \square \rightarrow 106.5 \text{ kg} + 4 \text{ kg} = 110.5 \text{ kg}$

$1 \square \rightarrow 110.5 \text{ kg} \div 5 = 22.1 \text{ kg}$

Peter's weight is $2 \square \rightarrow 22.1 \text{ kg} \times 2 \text{ units} = 44.2 \text{ kg}$

Peter weighs **44.2 kg.**

- -

17. At Big Al's restaurant, three cheeseburgers and two orders of fries cost $5.60. Four cheeseburgers and three orders of fries cost $7.80. How much does a single cheeseburger and a single order of fries each cost separately?

$5.60

$7.80

Each cheeseburger costs **$1.20**

Each French fry costs **$1.00.**

The difference between the two orders is 1 cheeseburger and one French fry.

1 cheeseburger and 1 fry = $7.80 - $5.60
                        = $2.20

2 cheeseburger and 2 fries = $2.20 + $2.20
                          = $4.40

1 cheeseburger = $5.60 − $4.40
              = $1.20

Since 1 cheeseburger + 1 fry   = $2.20
And 1 cheeseburger   = $1.20
THEN 1 French fry   = $2.20 - $1.20
                               = $1.00

13755115R00080